ASK

FOR THE

RAIN

ASK

FOR THE

RAIN

RECEIVING YOUR INHERITANCE OF
REVIVAL & OUTPOURING

COMPILED BY LARRY SPARKS

DESTINY IMAGE® PUBLISHERS, INC.

P.O. Box 310, Shippensburg, PA 17257-0310

"Promoting Inspired Lives."

This book and all other Destiny Image and Destiny Image Fiction books are available at Christian bookstores and distributors worldwide.

Cover design by Prodigy Pixel

For more information on foreign distributors, call 717-532-3040.

Reach us on the Internet: www.destinyimage.com.

ISBN 10: 0-7684-1074-6

ISBN 13 TP: 978-0-7684-1074-7

ISBN 13 eBook: 978-0-7684-1075-4

For Worldwide Distribution, Printed in the U.S.A.

1 2 3 4 5 6 7 8 / 20 19 18 17 16

DEDICATION

I dedicate this work to the fathers and mothers of revival. You have made it impossible for us to settle for any vision of the Christian life that does not involve a radical experience *with* and powerful demonstration *of* the fullness of the Holy Spirit.

And I dedicate this work to the sons and daughters of God that all of creation is waiting for.

You are not waiting for revival.

Revival is waiting for you.

I believe you have what it takes to accept this invitation and change the world.

CONTENTS

FOREWORD *by Lou Engle*..............................9

PREFACE   WHAT IS REVIVAL?...............................13

CHAPTER 1   A JOURNEY OF HUNGER............................17

CHAPTER 2   ASK FOR THE RAIN................................25

HOLY DISCONTENTMENT...33

CHAPTER 3   HOLY DISCONTENTMENT
              by Dr. Michael L. Brown..............................35

CHAPTER 4   THE ANSWER TO ANCIENT CRIES
              by Bill Johnson 45

SEND THE RAIN!...63

CHAPTER 5   THE CRY FOR GOD'S GLORY
              by John Kilpatrick 65

CHAPTER 6   HE'S DONE IT BEFORE; HE CAN DO IT AGAIN
              by Tommy Tenney 79

REVIVAL PRAYER...91

CHAPTER 7   PRAYER FOR REVIVAL IN THE CHURCH
              by James Goll..93

CHAPTER 8   THE SECRET PLACE
              by Banning Liebscher.................................111

WHEN HEAVEN BREAKS OUT 129

CHAPTER 9   THERE IS MORE
               by Corey Russell 133

CHAPTER 10   DON'T DIE BESIDE THE ARK
               by Larry Sparks.. 143

CHAPTER 11   LIVING OUT OF YOUR BOX
               by Don Nori Sr. 153

STEWARDING REVIVAL FOR INCREASE..................... 163

CHAPTER 12   EXPANDING THE THRONE ZONE
               by Tommy Tenney 165

CHAPTER 13   THIS PRESENT REVIVAL
               by Bill Johnson 183

CHAPTER 14   LIVING WATER, RUSHING RIVER................. 199

CONCLUSION   READY FOR THE RAIN............................ 203

FOREWORD
Foreword by Lou Engle

I am so happy to write the foreword to this book compiled by Larry Sparks, *Ask for The Rain*. These women and men he has gathered to write are not those who just talk about revival. They have seen revival, they're in revival and they are longing for more. Revival is God's arrival! And though we rejoice in what we have already received in the provision of Christ, we yet long for the full equipping of the Apostles, Prophets, Pastors, Preachers, and Teachers - the five-fold ministries who will bring us into experiential wonder of the fullness of the Son of God. The message of these five-fold friends of the body in this book will help us move forward to that great goal.

There has been much discussion about how we have everything in Christ and how we are now in revival. It's true and yet in the great expanse of the hidden glories of Christ yet undiscovered, we reach out and cry for more.

Years ago when I was still a young believer, Arthur Wallis, the father of the Charismatic movement in Great Britain, was speaking at our church gathering. As I listened to him there was a wrestling in my soul because though I had already received the baptism of the Holy Spirit I felt greatly dissatisfied with my experience of that baptism.

Wallis, in one of his books, mentions how tongues is what we promise and tongues is what we get now, but in the Acts of the Apostles, <u>power</u> was promised and <u>power</u> is what they got. That statement epitomized my inward struggle. After the meeting, Arthur Wallis was speaking to a group of people and I, brooding in my present plight, whispered to God, "Please have everybody leave Arthur so I can ask him about my dilemma." And immediately everybody left and Arthur just stood there alone. I walked up to him and said, "I am dissatisfied with my baptism of the Holy Spirit." He answered with a question: "Well, did you receive anything when you received the baptism?" I answered in the affirmative and again he responded, "Rejoice in what you have received but never stop hungering for more, for I too am a candidate for a greater baptism of the Holy Spirit."

How refreshing is the 'already' and the 'not yet'. And the not yet is why God raises up prophets. This is the plight of the prophet: having seen, he pulls what he has seen from the future down into the present through his passion, prayers and sacrifice. Having pulled it down, the body rejoices in its fresh revelation. Then the prophet begins seeing and dreaming again and while all others rejoice, he longs and groans again for a greater dimension of the fullness of Him who fills all in all.

That is why fasting is so critical to the body of Christ in these days. For while the bridegroom is still in heaven, the bride longs, fasts and creates a gravitational pull on the one who remains in heaven until He can remain no longer. But He does come, even now pulled by the divine hunger of the church. He comes with times of refreshing from The Lord.

I love the title of Larry Sparks' book, *Ask for the Rain*. Years ago in Pasadena, California I lost two of my favorite books. One was by Arthur Wallis called *The Day of Thy Power*, earlier titled *Rain From Heaven*. The other book was *Shaping History Through Prayer and Fasting* by Derek Prince. I couldn't find these books anywhere and I found myself groaning all day long saying, "I have to find those books." I was actually being drawn by a chapter in Prince's book entitled *Fasting Precipitates the Latter Rain.* In Joel 2, it states that after the fast, God promises to send the early and the latter rain. In essence, Joel 2 leads to Acts 2. It was such a strange day that I would find myself travailing with longing for these books. I wanted God to give me a sign that the fasting was bringing the rain of revival. That night I preached in Lancaster, California at my friend Joe Sweet's church. As I sat in his office that evening preparing for my preaching, he suddenly got up from his chair and walked over to the bookshelf. He reached into his bookshelf knowing nothing of my groaning and pulls out the book *The Day of Your Power/ Rain From Heaven* by Arthur Wallis. "I think you're looking for this book," he amazingly said to me. I shook at this sign.

The next morning I was teaching a prophetic class and before the meeting a brother came up to me and said that a man had met him early that morning at the Anaheim Vineyard and gave him a book saying, "Lou is looking for this right now." You guessed it; it was *Shaping History Through Prayer and Fasting* by Derek Prince. For 20 years I've locked onto this amazing window to heaven.

As the church longs for God, as she fasts and she prays, as she steps out in signs and wonders, as she blesses all the streams of the body of Christ, the rains begin to fall. I can hear the sound of a mighty rain. As you read the stories of these men and women in this book and as you tune your heart to the symphony of their song, you too will begin to hear the sounds of a mighty rain. Even now as I write this foreword, the 110th anniversary of the Azusa Street Revival is hurtling toward us. From 1909 to 1913 William Seymour, an African American man who contended to open up heaven and washed away the color line in the blood, prophesied that in 100 years a revival far eclipsing Azusa would come. Maria Woodworth-Etter, while in Chicago in 1913, proclaimed the same word. I'm in connection with a Nigerian pastor, Reverend Mossy, who has mobilized tens of thousands of believers in prayer for the last three years in Africa and Europe for the fulfillment of that prophecy. It's time to pray for the rain in the time of the latter rain. Then shall the great harvest spring forth in our nations and in every tribe and tongue. As the harvest ripens, pray for The Lord of the Harvest to thrust laborers into the world-wide harvest field. Let it rain.

—LOU ENGLE

WHAT IS REVIVAL?

Revival is not locked up in the heavens, waiting for enough desperate cries and persistent prayers to pull it down. This sounds spiritual, but is theologically and fundamentally *incorrect*.

Revival is not merely an event, church service, conference or special gathering.

Revival is not simply a season of heightened spiritual activity.

Revival is not even a *time* of visitation—and then back to "business as usual."

Revival is meant to *redefine* business as usual.

Revival, at its very core, is the dynamic demonstration of New Testament Christianity.

Without hype. Without pollution. Without compromise.

Jesus Christ being unveiled and revealed in His people, through the power of the Holy Spirit.

Revival involves a divine visitation of God's manifest Presence that produces a sustained habitation of His glory, both within and upon His people.

Revival challenges business as usual.

Revival confronts old wineskins, obsolete traditions, and outdated methods.

Revival calls the community of God to be otherworldly.

Revival compels you to be hungrier than your history.

Revival is a continuous river of Holy Spirit outpouring that has been flowing since the Day of Pentecost.

Revival is normal, supernatural Christianity in action and demonstration.

Revival is every Christ-follower walking in the fullness of the Holy Spirit's power.

Revival involves entire households, cities and regions being shaken by an overwhelming awareness of the manifest Presence of God.

In fact, *revival*—for all intensive purposes—is *not* God's perfect will for His people; it's the divine remedy to bring His people back to Heaven's perfect will.

Revival summons backsliders out of their spiritual wildernesses and ushers them into the very encounter their hearts were desperately longing for.

Revival sounds every siren throughout the hallways of hell, serving notice to a defeated satan that an activated, empowered and anointed body of Christ is returning to God's original blueprint—a Kingdom people who operate in purity and power.

Revival opens eyes to the supreme, limitless reality of *"Your Kingdom come...on earth as it is in Heaven,"* and that Jesus did not build comfortable perimeters or restrictive boundaries around *The Lord's Prayer.*

Revival reminds Christ-followers of the keys of Kingdom authority that they *already* carry—to bind what has been already bound in Heaven and release what has already been released in Heaven.

Truth be told, the community of God is not waiting for revival; revival is waiting for *whosoever will.*

Revival waits for an intercessory voice who says "Amen" to every promise that Heaven has already said *yes* to.

Revival waits for the one who *stops* praying, "Lord, rend the Heavens," and instead, starts praying and living as though Heaven has been open for business since the Day of Pentecost.

Revival waits for the individual or community whose hunger trumps their history: Regardless of where they have come from, what they have been taught or what their spiritual context had informed them, they are desperate enough to press beyond the past and move toward the fullness of what Scripture promises and the Spirit makes available, even at the risk of discomfort and rejection.

Revival waits for the eyes that are seeing what has been clear all along—it's raining. We are living in the time of outpouring. It's not reserved for one day, *someday,* nor was it exclusive to the past.

The "Great Last Days Revival" began on the Day of Pentecost... and *has been continuing* ever since.

The Heavens opened two thousands years ago...and the River of God *has been flowing* ever since that historic outpouring.

We are not waiting for the rain of Heaven.

We are living in the *time of rain.*

Why aren't we seeing this revival rain in a greater demonstration or outpouring? Simple answer.

We're asking God to send what He has *already sent.*

We're begging God to do what He has *already done.*

I repeat, *it's raining.* Why aren't we seeing rain released?

Because the very ones who carry the rain *within them* are gazing Heavenward, praying for Heaven to send down what has already been released and deposited.

We're praying, begging, and contending for what we have already been granted sacred stewardship of and unlimited access to.

We're asking God to send down what He wants to *send out*.

Yes, we should still persistently ask God to send His rain of revival.

Only now, it's not prayer emerging from a place of lack; it's a cry of hunger coming from a place of fullness... that desires increase.

It's not an empty people speaking to the Father, praying like deprived orphans when they are really sons and daughters with a full inheritance.

It's not about asking God to send down more of the Holy Spirit; we're asking God to help us live our lives in such a way that the Spirit is granted permission to be released *through us* in a greater demonstration. It's not about more of God coming down from Heaven; it's about more of God coming out of His people and being visibly manifested in the earth.

We begin our journey by awakening to this essential truth: The rain of revival has already been poured out *to us* so that we can cry out for an even *greater demonstration* of God's power and Presence to be poured out *through us*.

It all begins and ends with hunger.

CHAPTER 1

A JOURNEY OF HUNGER

Blessed are you who hunger now,
for you will be satisfied.
—LUKE 6:21, NIV

Every chapter you are about to read is purposed to do one simple thing—so awaken your hunger for God that you *move* past where you presently are and joyfully voyage into the depths of the Father. Pilgrimage into unexperienced realms of the Kingdom. Sojourn into new places of prayer. Run toward the higher ground of the sure Word. Plunge into the refreshing spring of Holy Spirit.

This book features writings from some of the most revolutionary revivalists and reformers of our day. Even so, none of these individuals seeks after greatness. The underlying characteristic of each voice represented in the forthcoming pages is simply *hunger*.

As leaders in the body of Christ, it can be tempting to "coast." Coast on ministry accolades. Coast on church growth methods. Coast on attendance. Coast on status. Coast on best-selling books. Coast on a thriving congregation. Coasting basically says that complacency is preferred over increased Kingdom demonstration. To coast in ministry or in our personal walks with God, we are choosing a certain place to "level off" at. We choose to go "this far and no more." We choose to be okay with what we know and what we've seen.

Maybe this describes you—or at least, you can relate to this "coasting" season at some point in your spiritual journey. We have all been there, to one degree or another. God is not mad at the "coasters." By no means. There is a greater issue than "coasting" in our walk with God; it's refusing to respond to His summons to move *beyond* where we are.

Read revival history, both historic and contemporary. Chances are, you are going to meet a bunch of former "coasters" who embraced a certain level of Christianity as their "normal." They selected a place of comfortability, stopped there, and decided to live in that level. The stories and various contexts are very different, but the next part is the unifying common denominator: *God comes down...* and usually, this visitation begins on a very deep, intimate, personal level before it impacts an entire church, let alone cities and nations.

HUNGER: YOUR DOORWAY INTO ANOTHER DIMENSION

I will list three contemporary revival leaders and provide a brief summary of their unique journeys of spiritual hunger. Even though each individual has a distinctive story, the theme is absolutely consistent: Hunger drove them into another dimension of God-encounter.

John Kilpatrick was an esteemed Assemblies of God pastor in Pensacola, FL. According to Kilpatrick, he had it made. A great family. A church who loved and respected him. A thriving television ministry. Onlookers would consider Kilpatrick a fine example of successful ministry. What they would not know is that, on the inside, the man was broken. He was aching for more. He would drive over to the Pensacola church sanctuary in the middle of the night, lay prostrate across the pews, and bellow out undignified intercessory groans, crying out for more of God. On Father's Day, 1995, the Brownsville Revival broke out and nations have been touched by this outpouring. Hunger drove Pastor Kilpatrick to a place of utter desperation. He was not begging God to send revival; it was far past that. He wanted his life, his church and his community to actually become saturated by the Presence of God that history and Scripture claimed were available. He pressed in until what was invisible became visible.

Randy Clark was a small-town Baptist pastor who had a growing local church. In the midst of his success, he found himself thinking: "God, thank You that I am not a liberal theologian—I believe you actually performed the miracles written in the Bible. God, thank You that I am not a cessationist—I believe that You still work miracles today." God's response was not quite what Randy expected. Instead of affirming his statements, the Lord basically said, "So what?" In essence, Randy believed in biblical realities that he was not *experiencing*. It's one thing to believe in miracles; it's another thing to walk in the miraculous. As a result of this experience, and others like it, God took Randy Clark on a journey of hunger that moved him past discomfort, into a series of supernatural encounters that unlocked healing, spiritual gifts, and ultimately, positioned him to be the key fire starter for 1994's Toronto Blessing, that has impacted the world—and is continuing to this day. His ministry, Global Awakening, is discipling Christians across the earth, empowering them to walk in God's supernatural power in their everyday lives. Hunger escorted a midwestern Baptist pastor into a lifestyle of revival that has shaken the nations.

Bill Johnson pastored a community of everyday people in the mountains of Weaverville, CA. For many years, the Johnson family was quite happy tending to their church, raising their family, and stewarding the ministry God had granted to them. Bill's problem was that he had read about the great miracles of God throughout revival history. In fact, he had tasted a measure of this power in his own life and ministry, but not to the degree he knew was available. Then, Johnson had an electrifying three-night-long encounter with God. In no way can my secondhand recounting of this experience do it justice, so I encourage you to seek out his testimony for yourself. Rather than focusing on *what happened*, I am more interested in *why* it happened. Bill's heart was postured through hunger to receive a destiny-defining encounter with the Holy Spirit. His cry? "God, I want more of You at any cost." Bill's hunger did not convince an unwilling God to move; rather, it brought Bill to a place where he could access more of God because he was willing to align his life and church with the Holy Spirit's present movement, no matter what the cost. And it would cost him tremendously. But what Bill Johnson and Bethel Church have experienced in exchange infinitely overshadows the cost.

These are three examples among the multitudes of men and women, old and young, who have allowed their hunger for more of God to move them beyond familiarity, out from their history and into their destiny. I could not even begin to provide you with a list of names—dating back to the first three hundred years of the church—of those who pressed past the restrictions of religion and the boundaries of formalism, and aligned their lives with the continuous, refreshing flow of the River of God.

Evan Roberts cried out for many years, hungry to experience a fresh demonstration of God's power in his community. He realigned his entire life to position himself to experience revival. In 1904, the Welsh Revival broke out and radically impacted the entire nation. It is believed that over 100,000 people were converted to Christianity because of this revival.

William Seymour, one of the key pioneers of American Pentecostalism, was a one-eyed black man living in a time of heinous racism. He couldn't sit in Charles Parham's Bible classes, so he sat outside and listened through the door. He preached the baptism of the Holy Spirit and got locked out of his church. In fact, he preached the "more" of God—Spirit baptism—without compromise, even though he personally did not experience it immediately. He tirelessly preached on the Spirit's fire and power *until* what was visible only in Scripture became experiential in his life and the community at the Azusa Street Mission. This determined spiritual hunger was catalytic in birthing the Azusa Street Revival of 1906, which ultimately produced Pentecostalism as we know it.

THE CATALYST OF CRISIS

Crisis has historically led so many to cry out for more of God. *What is this crisis?* Not necessarily tragic events or disaster; the crisis I am describing is that gaping chasm existing between visible reality and Scriptural reality, what's presently seen and what is biblically available. Throughout the ages, there have been those who refused to conform to the status quo of what was visible. This crisis of faith pushed them past status quo Christianity and catapulted them into "dangerous" depths of supernatural encounter. These spiritual crisis moments are dangerous, not because they are heretical or unscriptural, but because they threaten the way it's *always been done.* Crisis threatens the comfortable, demanding those who have fallen into the lull of comfort to consider their ways. God is truly raising up reformational voices once again who are calling: "Awake, O sleeper, and arise from the dead, and Christ will shine on you" (Eph. 5:14). They are calling forth the invisible realities of Heaven to confront unbiblical realities on earth.

The visible reality could have been the buying/selling of indulgences, certificates that—when purchased—could provide loved ones with relief from the holding tank of purgatory. Reformers like Martin Luther, John Calvin, and Ulrich Zwingli confronted such fallacies, as they were gripped by the biblical realities of "by grace, through faith."

The visible reality could have been a dry church, where the Holy Spirit became limited to being a theological agent of regeneration, not a dynamic Person who released Kingdom power. Leaders like Charles

Parham and William Seymour confronted this crisis with the emergence of the Pentecostal movement in the 1900's.

The visible reality could have been a powerless people, where Christianity simply became a ticket into Heaven rather than a dynamic collaboration with God to bring Heavenly realities into the earthly realm. Leaders like John Wimber confronted this by reminding every single Christ-follower of their empowerment to heal the sick, cast out demons, and operate in gifts of the Holy Spirit.

We can never allow the visible reality to become our definition of Christianity *when* the visible reality is in opposition to the biblical reality. This produces status quo Christians at best; immoral and carnal Christians at worst. Revival is not a happy thing for those settled in a status quo existence. Status quo Christianity continues to "go with the flow," even when the flow was actually running contrary to the River of God. Even though the masses have often been content to settle for shallow-water spirituality, certain men and women have historically been gripped by this crisis of seeing the realities available in Scripture (or in church history) and calling the church of their generation to contend for those invisible realities to be released.

The good news is this: *it's raining and no one is safe!* For the wandering backsliders, I believe you are going to experience springs of refreshing in your wilderness seasons. God will meet you. Not religion. Not rules and regulations. Not your past prejudices or upbringing. I believe the Holy Spirit is moving in this hour to *meet* people in ways like never before.

YOU ARE BEING SUPERNATURALLY SETUP!

You are being setup! Truth be told, this book is chapter after chapter of intentional setup. Having more information and knowledge is not sufficient in the hour in which we live. We are informed, taught and educated to a fault sometimes. Rather than receiving more information, I believe you are going to experience what Catherine Booth referred to as "burning words."

What you read is going to burn within your heart and ignite a fresh hunger for God, unlike you have ever experienced. It's not because any of our words are special; it's because each author has positioned their offering in such a way that, more than simply presenting a good piece of writing, they were intent on allowing the Holy Spirit to overshadow them and, in turn, they simply stewarded what He was communicating. The key to positioning yourself for an encounter with God is being open to what the Holy Spirit is saying and doing. Allow Him to move in your heart without restraint.

The name Catherine Booth may not be familiar to you, but perhaps you have heard of her husband, William Booth—founder of the Salvation Army. Due to the nature of their ministry, William and Catherine found themselves traveling a lot. Even though this woman heard some of the greatest sermons from some of the most notable pastors and leaders, she still cried out: "Burning words! That's what I'm looking for. I travel all around, and I hear oratory; I hear clever preaching. But what I'm searching for is something that will burn my heart like the men on the road to Emmaus."

> *They said to each other, "Did not our hearts burn within us while he talked to us on the road, while he opened to us the Scriptures?"* (Luke 24:32)

As you read the insights, testimonies and Scriptures contained in this book, I pray that your heart would burn. More Christian rhetoric is not the solution for this urgent hour—burning words are. We need words that ignite our hearts to relentlessly pursue and experience the *more* of God.

I pray that, just like those disciples on the road to Emmaus, your heart would burn as you go on this journey. Most certainly, you will be introduced to a number of different voices. I encourage you, don't allow the varying writing styles or different methods of presentation to distract you. Simply know this: Each distinct voice of revival represented in this book is one who is not writing about the subject as a researcher or teacher, but rather, providing eyewitness testimony and revelation from the standpoint of an active participant. These leaders have tasted the power of the age to come. They have experienced revival and renewal firsthand, unlike many in this present generation. This doesn't make them superstars; it just keeps them hungry. So in essence, you are reading words written *by the hungry, for the hungry.*

May this hunger to experience and release the *rain of revival* permeate and transform your life!

CHAPTER 2

ASK FOR THE RAIN

Ask the Lord for rain in the time of the latter rain.
—ZECHARIAH 10:1, NKJV

*I*t's raining. In fact, it has been raining since the Day of Pentecost. From that sovereign moment in history onward, Heaven has been opened and the Holy Spirit has been released. The great need of the present hour is not to beseech God, crying out for another Pentecost. The first one was absolutely sufficient. We don't need more God out of Heaven; we need more God out of us, the church. We need to see the outworking, the demonstration and the manifestation of what every believer carries—the power of the resurrected Christ.

HOW DO WE RESPOND TO THE RAIN?

The passage in Zechariah illustrates a principle more than it makes a definitive prophetic statement. I am not claiming that Zechariah 10:1, in its context, refers to the rain of revival. On the other hand, I do believe that Scripture passages like this do give us illustrations and pictures of how the Kingdom of God operates. What is the appropriate respond to the rain of outpouring? *Ask for more.* When you cease pressing in to experience more of God, the very thing we labeled as "revival" in a former season can become religion in the next.

What was a flowing, vibrant revival river in one season can actually became a stagnant pond in the next season. How is this even possible? Simple. When we decide to cease discovering the fullness of God, we camp out in a comfortable place. Comfort prevents us from further exploration. It's the hunger for further exploration of God that keeps people postured to experience the increase of revival. Revival is not this mystical, sovereign thing that happens at periodic, arbitrary times in history. While there is a sovereign element to revival, I find that—more often than not—it's the byproduct of a man or woman who becomes discontent living in a previous level of "glory" with God.

The way things presently are can no longer satisfy the parched soul. These people catch glimpses of *greater* downpour. Even though they might have experienced rain in some measure, they somehow taste something greater. This often comes through catching a glimpse of these "greater" realities presented in Scripture, or hearing testimony of someone who tasted the "greater." Either way, the testimony of *greater things* instills within a hungry heart the desire to keep pressing on for increase. Increased outpouring. Increased revival rain. Increased activity of the Holy Spirit. Rather than trying to convince God to send the increase, these people have actually experienced this greater demonstration of revival because they aligned themselves to get caught up in the ever-increasing flow of the River of God.

When revival becomes a comfortable place, and we cease asking for *more*, then what was a fresh, dynamic expression of the Holy Spirit at one time can become absolutely drained of Heaven's life.

The Spirit of God is a moving Spirit. He is ever escorting the body of Christ into deeper places, as there always more of God to know and experience. Heaven's travel plan for your life, individually, and for the church collectively, is "glory to glory." How do we keep journeying on this road, *from glory to glory*? We live gripped by the reality that consumed the lives of men and women throughout the centuries, transforming ordinary people into revivalists who saw movements birthed, cities transformed and nations touched by the glory of God. Revivalists are born in the tension between *glory to glory*. Yes, there is glory in a former season or expression of outpouring; however, as wonderful as that is, there is more. There is increase. God is greater than the last season of awakening and period of revival. Could it be that we have not seen consistent, sustained revival because we are expecting God to continue things *as is* when in fact, He deliberately and intentionally wants to turn up the heat.

Our skewed picture of a sustained move of God is simply seeing what happened at the beginning of an outpouring continue without interruption. This is not God's agenda for revival, as His objective is increasing Heaven's territory and jurisdiction on earth—the key word being "increase." As long as we are navigating revival correctly, stagnancy and sameness will be impossible. The only thing God will do with an individual or community who truly desires to experience Him in a greater, deeper way, is increase the manifestation of His Presence. This is why revivalists are birthed in the tension between glories. Even though they celebrate the glory released in the former, early days of revival, they recognize that there is only more to come and they posture themselves accordingly.

They are not content to become comfortable with the rain of revival. When the Spirit of God is moving, they desire to both steward His present activity along with crying out for increase. This is not greedy; it's Kingdom. One thing we read about the operation of God's Kingdom, starting back in the Old Testament, is that it is a reign of increase: "Of the increase of his government and peace there shall be no end" (Isa. 9:7, KJV). We should be crying out for the increase and expansion of God's reign and dominion *on earth as it is in Heaven* until we see earth visibly transformed by the realities of Heaven. The key to seeing the supernatural resources of Heaven released on earth is remaining *spiritually mature.*

WHAT DOES TRUE SPIRITUAL MATURITY LOOK LIKE?

Spiritual maturity is not measured by the number of degrees accumulated or quantity of doctrine memorized. While seminary education is helpful and an understanding of Christian doctrine is valuable, the great secret to ever-increasing spiritual maturity is given to us by the apostle Paul.

> *Not that I have already obtained this or am already perfect, but I press on to make it my own, because Christ Jesus has made me his own. Brothers, I do not consider that I have made it my own. But one thing I do: forgetting what lies behind and straining forward to what lies ahead, I press on toward the goal for the prize of the upward call of God in Christ Jesus. Let those of us who are mature think this way, and if in anything you think otherwise, God will reveal that also to you* (Phil. 3:12-15).

If anyone had the right to stagnate in a former level of glory, it was Paul. In fact, he was the writer who gave us the language of this "glory to glory" journey in Second Corinthians 3:18. He certainly had spiritual bragging rights, coming from the background that he did and being educated in the manner that he was.

Even still, Paul was a man who recognized that he had *not* obtained the fullness of what God had made available. *There was more* and Paul was absolutely intent on seeking it. Experiencing it. Apprehending it. This same quest is available to us today. Recognizing this is what keeps us asking for *more* in the time of outpouring. This is exactly what Paul was doing in this section of his letter to the Philippians. He defined maturity as "forgetting what lies behind and straining forward to what lies ahead" (Phil. 3:13). He pressed into God. He strained to experience greater glimpses. He moved forward in spite of an impressive theological knowledge bank. Paul's example is your invitation today. If you want to experience revival and see an increase of God's supernatural activity on earth, it begins by defining true Christian maturity as a lifelong quest to knowing, tasting, and experiencing more of God—and ever recognizing that there is more of this God to know and experience.

How do you live mindful of the expansiveness and largeness and magnitude of God? Start by praying some new revival prayers. Paul never spent his time praying for God to send something new down from Heaven. Even though I cherish so many of the songs, old and new, that speak of some fresh outpouring coming *down* from above, it is important for us to diligently search the Scriptures and see exactly how disciples of old kept their "revival fire" burning for God.

Perhaps the greatest revival prayer I can think of is shared in Ephesians 1, where Paul gives us a glimpse into the language of his prayer life:

> *That the God of our Lord Jesus Christ, the Father of glory, may give you the Spirit of wisdom and of revelation in the knowledge of him, having the eyes of your hearts enlightened, that you may know what is the hope to which he has called you, what are the riches of his glorious inheritance in the saints, and what is the immeasurable greatness of his power toward us who believe, according to the working of his great might* (Eph. 1:17-19).

What is the key to experientially—not merely intellectually—knowing *the rights of his glorious inheritance in the saints* and *the immeasurable greatness of his power toward us who believe*? After all, this sounds like revival language! We want to know the rights He has given to us, His children and saints, so that we can unlock our glorious inheritance. We want to be awakened to the immeasurable greatness of the power He has deposited into us through the indwelling Holy Spirit. As these rich discoveries are made, the church will, by default, operate in the power of revival—which is basically normal Christianity. An absolutely glorious prospect.

So what is the secret? Review Paul's language in his Ephesians 1 prayer. Nowhere do you see him asking God to send something new down from Heaven. We don't pray for open heavens; we pray for open eyes. Heaven has been opened since Pentecost; we need to ask God to help us open our eyes to see what He *already* made available to us, and in turn, ask for wisdom on how to access, experience, walk in, and release it.

MORE RAIN, LORD!

I remember being really bothered by some of the oft repeated "revival phrases" that were popularized during the 1990's. Perhaps one of the most frequent phrases was "more, Lord!" I found myself getting agitated over this language, whether it was delivered in the form of a prayer, declaration or a song. For the life of me, I could not figure out why we were praying for "More love, more power, more of *You* in my life," when in fact, we already had the Holy Spirit. How can you have more of an infinite God? It didn't make sense to me. That was my main issue, right there. Since this did not make sense to me, I embraced the "know it all spirit," in which I wrote off this "more, Lord" language as unscriptural and spiritually immature. I am amazed at how God uses the very things we are often so vehemently against to humble us.

Biblically, I became absolutely convinced that there was no Holy Spirit 2.0 or upgraded version. This is absolutely true. Yet, there was something that the "more, Lord" people were experiencing that I was *not*—God! They obviously had something right. Yet, I was convinced that, in some way, I was correct as well since we should not be asking

God to send another Spirit down from Heaven. Along this journey, I discovered a rich synergy of both perspectives that brought me to the conclusion I have outlined in this chapter: When it's raining, *ask for more.* Even though we have received the fullness of God living within us, there is more of Him to experience and demonstrate through yielded and hungry lives.

There is no more Holy Spirit for God to send down from Heaven; however, there is *much more* Holy Spirit that needs to be sent out from us. From me. From you. From the church. The Spirit of God has been given a home in our mortal bodies of flesh. This was sovereignly orchestrated by God's divine design. I may never understand why the Holy One found it fit to entrust His very Spirit—one who is identified as *Holy*—to an often unholy people. A people who, though saved and Spirit-filled, often still gravitate toward uncleanness and sin. This absolutely confounds me. Yet, it's in this confounding reality that I can only say, "Thank You, Jesus, for giving me Your Spirit! I'm not worthy of so glorious and so holy of a gift, but You declared me to be!"

So what do we do with this quest for more of the God we have received in full? How do we engage Him? Pursue Him? Cry out for *more* of the One who already dwells within us? It all comes down to stepping into a greater revelation of our identity as a people filled with and possessed by the Holy Spirit. The whole of created order is actually awaiting the unveiling of such a people, according to Romans 8:

> *For the creation waits with eager longing for the revealing of the sons of God. For the creation was subjected to futility, not willingly, but because of him who subjected it, in hope that the creation itself will be set free from its bondage to corruption and obtain the freedom of the glory of the children of God. For we know that the whole creation has been groaning together in the pains of childbirth until now* (Romans 8:19-22).

Creation has long awaited the anointed sons and daughters who carry supernatural, redemptive solutions that will restore what was lost when the world was "subjected to futility" in Eden.

It's not about who *we* are; it's about Who He is in us and through us. The church has often gotten lost in the question of identity, either reducing Christ-followers to lowly "sinners saved by grace," on the hyper-humble end, or people who can do anything and everything, on the spiritually prideful end. Both perspectives are perversions of the truth. It's true, we *were* depraved sinners, incapable of making movement toward God, who were saved by grace. Grace did it all. It saved us and created within us an awareness of the very need for salvation.

Now that we are saved, the Spirit of the risen Christ lives within us. This revelation should give us supernatural confidence, not in ourselves, but in the One who made our bodies His temple. If God is really inside of us, then everywhere we walk, we carry the rule, reign and administration of the Kingdom of Heaven.

The whole of creation has been groaning in the pains of childbirth...until now. Even though the land is dry and weary, and it seems like there is no water, there is a solution: Revival. And you carry it!

HOLY
DISCONTENTMENT

There is no revival without a divine discontentment. Heaven is ready and waiting. God has sovereignly chosen to make the Holy Spirit and His fullness available to "whosoever." The problem is that many believers are living beneath their inheritance in Christ. Fortunately, there is a discontentment brewing among Jesus's followers.

Why does this discontentment exist? Because where we presently are and what we are currently experiencing is not the fullness of what Scripture claims is available in God. Holy discontentment is spiritually healthy because it keeps us pressing toward experientially knowing more of what God has made available. We don't just know it with our heads; we know it through firsthand experience, crying out as revivalists have throughout the ages: "Lord, there must be more. I'm not content just reading about it; I want to taste it. I want to walk in it. I want to see Your power demonstrated through me!" Even in times of revival and outpouring, holy discontentment keeps the hungry crying out for "more." Even though it's raining in measure, there's more rain to be released.

Dr. Michael Brown is a contemporary general of revival. His voice adds a very unique perspective to this volume, as he represents a unique blend of revivalist, theologian, and biblical scholar. He does not write from the position of a spectator, presenting a "wouldn't it be nice if revival happened" perspective. Dr. Brown experienced the fires of revival firsthand, from 1996-2000 during the Brownsville Revival in Pensacola, FL. Out of that revival, Dr. Brown pioneered FIRE School of Ministry which has been training, equipping and releasing Christian leaders across the globe.

The following chapter is adapted from two of Dr. Brown's landmark books on revival, *Whatever Happened to the Power of God* and *The Fire That Never Sleeps*.

CHAPTER 3

HOLY DISCONTENTMENT

Dr. Michael L. Brown

*O that in me the sacred fire might now
begin to glow, burn up the dross of base
desire, and make the mountains flow.*
—CHARLES WESLEY

What we are presently walking in is not all it is played up to be. It cannot possibly be the same brand of faith as that which shook the ancient world. If our God "is able to do immeasurably more than all we ask or imagine," why do we ask for so much according to His will and apparently receive so little (see Eph. 3:20)? Why do the imaginations and dreams we had when we were first saved seem like immature fantasies now?

WHERE ARE THE GREATER WORKS?

We talk about doing the "greater works" of Jesus, but let's be real—ten of us doing the same works of the Lord would challenge all of America overnight. (I wonder if there are even five of us who could handle such an anointing—along with all the media exposure—without letting it go to our heads.)

Preachers, can you be candid enough to stand up at your healing services and say, "If what we are seeing is a true reflection of the Lord, then He must be fickle, arbitrary, and relatively powerless!"

Evangelists, are you willing to boldly proclaim at your "revival" meetings, "If what we are experiencing is the fullness of the Spirit, then we ought to quit right now and go home!"

Pastors, will you express clearly to your flocks, "If the quality of life we are manifesting in the Lord is the best there is, then our churches are in trouble!"

Believers, do you have the courage to get alone with God and say to Him honestly, "If what I have is all the Christianity there is, then the thing is a fraud!"

God would be pleased with us if we did this. He was the One who said through His servant Malachi, "Oh, that one of you would shut the temple doors, so that you would not light useless fires on My altar!" (Mal. 1:10, NIV). That's right, useless fires—and God was the One who said so! He would rather that we close down the show if we won't clean up our acts. Why continue with our rituals if the Lord does not approve?

THE THIEF OF REVIVAL

Once more, these words are not purposed to bring condemnation. You, me—the entire Church—we all need to be called up higher. In fact, *higher* is that spiritual normal we are trying to get back to. The enemy of higher is mediocre. When it comes to the Gospel, mediocrity is often embraced when we mistakenly believe there is no place higher to go in God. This thought process in and of itself is a great deception that robs us of our cry for revival. Landscape-changing revival is birthed by a cry that sees *higher* and longs to bring one's spiritual experience into alignment with the possibilities seen in the New Testament.

The question is: Why are we satisfied with *useless fires* when the real, authentic, genuine, burning fire of God has been made readily available? Once again, I encourage you to let these words build up your spiritual tenacity, whether you are in full-time ministry or are a dissatisfied believer. We should embrace the following perspective: If I believe that where I am in my relationship with God is the be-all and end-all of my Christian experience, then there is something fraudulent about the faith I am professing.

Wouldn't it be glorious if ministers across the country said to their flocks on Sunday, "We're not having church today! We're not going on with an empty routine! No new programs or plans! We're going to confess our sins to God and acknowledge our spiritual bankruptcy. And we're going to stay here all morning and pray for revival."

What would happen to our country if congregations did this just one Sunday each month, without giving up or losing heart? The face of our nation would change.

WE MUST BECOME DESPERATE

We need to think of those we've preached to for years—with little sign of lasting victory in their lives—and cry out, "Where is the power of the Gospel?"

We need to remember all those who died of terrible sickness and disease—never receiving their expected healing—and cry out, "Where is the power of the Gospel?"

We need to walk the streets of our corrupt cities, looking at the addicts and alcoholics and prostitutes—in spite of churches on almost every street—and cry out, "Where is the power of the Gospel?"

We need to consider how the Mormons, Muslims, and other groups are aggressively infiltrating our communities—while our own feeble witnessing efforts lack convicting authority—and cry out, "Where is the power of the Gospel?"

We must force a crisis in our lives. *More of the same will only produce more of the same.*

Something fundamental, something basic, must change. Just building ourselves up with more faith, more consecration, more soul-winning, more Scripture meditation, or more love will not turn the tide. All of these things are good. They are necessary ingredients to our spiritual lives. But in and of themselves they cannot deliver us from our present rut unless we couple them with deep spiritual hunger.

Our whole orientation to spiritual things must be altered, and altered from the roots. *We don't need more methods and techniques. No! We need the Lord Himself to come down and lift us up. Nothing else will do.* And when we seek Him with all our heart and all our soul, when our very being aches with desire for His visitation, when we are consumed with hunger for His reality, when we radically cut back on other activities in order to seek His face, then we are ripe for transformation. Then the breakthrough will come. We can be immersed into the very nature and authority of the Lord.

How miserable it is that "the average Christian is so cold and so contented with his wretched condition that there is no vacuum of desire into which the blessed Spirit can rush in satisfying fullness."[1]

THE ROAD TO REVIVAL

What can we do to position ourselves to experience revival?

First, we need to *recognize our need*. We need to confront both our personal need and our spiritual need. Jesus rebukes the Laodicean church in Revelation 3:17, saying, "For you say, I am rich, I have prospered, and I need nothing, not realizing that you are wretched, pitiable, poor, blind, and naked."

This process might be uncomfortable but it is ultimately life-giving. We can never posture our hearts for revival if we refuse to acknowledge the dead areas in our personal lives and walk with the Lord.

Second, we need to *understand what God has done in the past*: "*I remember the days of old; I meditate on all that you have done; I ponder the work of your hands* (Ps. 143:5).

We need to read about revival in Scripture, study historic outpourings, familiarize ourselves with the past moves of God, and connect ourselves with what God is doing in other parts of the world. We should listen and watch—do whatever we can to expose ourselves to what God has done and is doing. By studying the testimony of God's mighty acts, these stories stir hunger in our hearts and create fresh faith. The God who moved *then* can surely *move again*. The God who is mightily at work in a different part of the world is the same God in our country and nation!

Even though the idea of positioning ourselves for the next great awakening may seem like a giant mountain to climb, we must start to take simple steps in the right direction. God is looking for those who will make the consistent, daily choices to obey Him, to follow His Word, to study His works, and to live transparently before Him.

I went through a personal spiritual crisis back in 1982. God began to convict me as people were praying for me. The Lord showed me that I had left my first love. At first this seemed strange. I was an active believer. I was a serious believer. I was committed in many ways, but I had greatly neglected personal prayer and devotion. My personal fire for the Lord was flickering out. I had greatly neglected just feasting on the Word as opposed to studying the original languages. God began to convict me for leaving my first love, just as the Church in Ephesus had (see Rev. 2:4). In the midst of this season, I started to recognize the distance I created between the Lord and me. I saw how far I had wandered from where I once was.

Even though I was still a committed believer, I was just a shell of who I used to be spiritually. I thought to myself, "I can fast and pray and I will be ablaze for a few days but then I'll quickly go back to the way I was." That was not going to work. I was up and down. I was inconsistent in my passion for the Messiah. Finally I said, "Here is what I can do. I can take a step in the right direction and take another step and take another step."

If you feel the same way, I want to encourage you to believe in the power of *one step*. You may feel as though you have wandered millions of miles away from God and from where you used to be. You might feel as though the chasm you created between you and the Lord is hopeless—that God is finished with you. This is a lie. One step on your end is all it takes to invite God in. You might have gone ten million miles from where you were. Just take *one step* in faith toward God and be confident that He has made the ten-million-mile journey that you could *never* make. Then take the next step and the next step, and before you know it, dramatic change will come in your life.

DISCONTENTMENT: YOUR KEY TO REVIVAL

Notable author of *My Utmost For His* Highest, Oswald Chambers, was not content with where he was, as his vacuum of hunger was too great. He came to the critical juncture that the Holy Spirit is beckoning you to:

> Those of you who know the experience (of the baptism of the Spirit), know very well how God brings one to the point of utter despair, and I got to the place where I did not care whether everyone knew how bad I was. I cared for nothing on earth, saving to get out of my present condition.
>
> At the end of a little meeting, after singing "Touch Me Again Lord," Chambers said: "I felt nothing, but I knew emphatically my time had come, and I rose to my feet. I had no vision of God, only a sheer, dogged determination

to take God at His Word and to prove this thing for myself. And I stood up and said so. That was bad enough, but what followed was ten times worse. After I sat down, the speaker, who knew me well, said, "That is very good of our brother. He has spoken like that as an example to the rest of you."

Up I got again and said, "I got up for no one's sake. I got up for my own sake. Either Christianity is a downright fraud, or I have not got hold of the right end of the stick." And then, and there, I claimed the gift of the Holy Spirit in dogged committal on Luke 11:13. I had no vision of Heaven or of angels. I had nothing. I was as dry and empty as ever, no power or realization of God, no witness of the Holy Spirit.[2]

But something supernatural *had* taken place. God had taken hold of his life. Four years later Chambers commented:

If the previous years had been Hell on earth, these four years have truly been Heaven on earth. Glory be to God, the last aching abyss of the human heart is filled to overflowing with the love of God. Love is the beginning, love is the middle, and love is the end. After He comes in, all you see is "Jesus only, Jesus ever."[3]

Looking back, Oswald Chambers could say, "The baptism of the Holy Ghost does not make you think of time or eternity; it is one amazing, glorious now.... It is no wonder that I talk so much about an altered disposition: God altered mine; I was there when He did it, and I have been there ever since."[4]

STIRRINGS OF SPIRITUAL OUTPOURING

Just as the Holy Spirit stirred Chambers's heart to experience personal revival, the Lord continues to perform such a work even today. The signs are all there!

I would like to take you back for a moment to the season just prior to the Brownsville Revival. For some years, I had been desperate for divine visitation and outpouring. I was absolutely convinced that revival was America's only hope. Motivated by this conviction, I had been preaching and writing about these themes for several years, beginning with my 1989 book *End of the American Gospel Enterprise*, 1990's *How Saved Are We?* and then 1991's *Whatever Happened to the Power of God?*

In March of 1995, I released the book *A Time for Holy Fire*. It concluded with the words "Are you ready?" I was convinced that something powerful was just waiting at the door. Revival was near! There was a stirring and the beginnings of a new outpouring, and I sensed it was right at the door, ready to break.

I don't see that same stirring today, but I see an inkling of it. I see the beginnings of it. I hear more and more people saying that we've got to have revival; we've got to seek God. More and more major Christian voices are speaking again about our desperate need for a great awakening. In my view, this was happening much more in the late 1980s and into the early '90s than it is now. But I see it rising again and that is an encouragement. I see that sense of desperation and urgency gripping the body of Christ once more.

With Brownsville specifically, I was not at the church prior to Revival. But I know Pastor John Kilpatrick reached a point of absolute desperation during which he would shut himself in the church building at night and pray for hours in the dark. He would cry out, "God, if you don't come and visit, I can't go on." That was the kind of hunger stirring in my heart. That was the hunger that was in evangelist Steve Hill's heart. Among all of us, that combined hunger and thirst was something very powerful. *God is the One who alone initiates spiritual hunger; it is up to us to respond to it.* He stirs our hearts to hunger, and as we respond He graciously comes to fill the hungry.

I don't see us at that desperate point right now, but I see us getting there, little by little. That's positive. The question is, are *you* willing to respond to His stirrings?

Are you willing to become consumed to the core of your being with desire for God?

Are you willing to let Him strip you of all confidence in the flesh until you get to the point of total dependence on Him?

Are you willing—in brokenness and humility—to stand out from the crowd that is apparently satisfied with leftover bread?

Are you willing to be emptied and emptied again so that God can fully fill you? The choice is entirely yours.

How far are you willing to go?

ENDNOTES

1. A. W. Tozer, *Born After Midnight* (Camp Hill, PA: Christian Publications, 1959), 22.

2. The account of Oswald Chambers's spiritual breakthrough is taken from Edwin F. Harvey and Lillian Harvey, *They Knew Their God*, vol. 3 (Hampton, TN: Harvey and Tait, 1988), 9-5-96.

3. Ibid.

4. Ibid.

Pastor Bill Johnson teaches that two essential keys to experiencing an increase of God's supernatural power in your life are humility and hunger. We cannot underestimate the value of these qualities. Consider the history of revival. Even in the last hundred-plus years, time after time, major outpourings of the Holy Spirit broke out among the poor—not simply those who were poor economically, but the poor in spirit.

Holy discontentment is not often birthed in the ivory towers of academia or among those who consider themselves theological masterminds. Learning and theology are to be prized, certainly, but not at the expense of crying out for a greater demonstration of God's power in our lives and in our communities. The very cry for something "greater" reveals lack on our end. We must be willing to confront our lack, no matter how well studied we are. Whether we own a financially prosperous business or have built a nationally renown mega-church, our blessings can become a curse if we allow them to convince us we are "full."

Bill Johnson is the best-selling author of titles like *When Heaven Invades Earth, Hosting the Presence,* and *Supernatural Power of a Transformed Mind.* When people hear of Bethel Church, they think of a significant worship movement that has emerged, a high frequency of signs, wonders, and miracles, and a dynamic church that is serving nations across the earth, equipping all Christ-followers to live in both purity and power. Bill could easily observe these accomplishments as his license to "coast" for the rest of his life. After all, he has experienced unprecedented measures of God's Presence and power at work in his life and among the Bethel community.

Yet, when you get to know Bill—personally, through his writing, or listening to his preaching—you are quickly introduced to a man who truly lives what he preaches. He exemplifies a life that is both humble and hungry. If anyone has experienced the "rain" of God, it's Pastor Bill. And yet, he is constantly asking for more. In humility, he recognizes that he hasn't experienced everything there is of God and in hunger, he pursues the "more" of God that is yet to be tasted, experienced, and released.

The following segment is taken from Bill's signature book, *Hosting the Presence.* It provides perspective on how to respond to our discontentment. The heavens have been opened; it's now time for spiritually hungry people to arise and draw out the resources that have been made abundantly available.

CHAPTER 4

THE ANSWER TO ANCIENT CRIES

Bill Johnson

The cries for God, some from the righteous and some from the unrighteous, have sounded through the ages. I grew up hearing there was a God-shaped vacuum in the heart of every person. I believe it.

This longing for God is seen in so many ways, including the drive to make things better in life. I've traveled all over the world. And one thing that exists in every people group I've seen is the desire to discover new things and make what exists better. This passion is firmly rooted in everyone.

God created us with desires and passions and the capacity to dream. All of these traits are necessary to truly make us like Him. With these abilities, we can discover more of God, our purpose in life, and the beauty and fullness of His Kingdom. When these abilities exist unharnessed by divine purpose, they take us to forbidden fruit. It was a risk God was willing to take in order to end up with His dream—those made in His image, who worship Him by choice, who carry His Presence into all the earth.

Isaiah represented the cry of all humanity when he prayed, *"Rend the heavens and come down!"* It was known somehow that the realities of Heaven and earth must be closer to each other. In this prayer, the cry for Heaven to influence earth had once again exploded from the heart. This time it was from a prophet. God had already set the stage to answer and instructed Isaiah to make the prayerful declaration. It was a prophetic word in the form of a prayer.

Heaven's answer came. The revelation and release of God's redemptive program is now unstoppable.

HEAVEN IS A PERSON

The water baptism of John was known as a baptism of repentance. That made Jesus's request of John to baptize Him strange and quite difficult to process. Jesus had no sin to repent of. But John's baptism was also a part of his announcement of the Kingdom being near. When John said the Kingdom was near, he was prophesying about what Jesus would manifest and release.

John knew he wasn't worthy to baptize Jesus. In fact, he confessed his need for the baptism that Jesus would bring—in the Holy Spirit and fire (see Matt. 3:11). But Jesus insisted. Being willing to do what you are not qualified to do is sometimes what qualifies you.

Jesus answered John's objection, *"Permit it at this time; for in this way it is fitting for us to fulfill all righteousness"* (Matt. 3:15, NASB). Righteousness was fulfilled in this act because here Jesus became the servant of all, identified with sinful humanity, and was now positioned to announce that the Kingdom of God is at hand. The announcement brought the release, as nothing happens in the Kingdom until first there is a declaration.

When Jesus was baptized in water, Heaven took notice. Here is an interesting description of this divine moment.

Immediately coming up out of the water, He saw the heavens opening, and the Spirit like a dove descending upon Him; and a voice came out of the heavens: "You are My beloved Son, in You I am well-pleased" (Mark 1:10-11, NASB).

Jesus saw the *heavens opening*. What had been promised through the ages had started. But no one expected this: Heaven invading earth through the humility of a man—the Son of God, the Son of Man.

The word *opening* means to *cleave, split*. It is translated as *opening*, *split*, and *tears* one time each, *divided* and *tear* two times each, and *torn* four times. Interestingly, it is the same word used to describe both the veil in the temple being *torn* and the rocks *splitting* open at Jesus's death, as Heaven and earth shook as a witness to the injustice of that moment—One so perfect dying for those who deserve death. *"And behold, the veil of the temple was torn in two from top to bottom; and the earth shook and the rocks were split"* (Matt. 27:51, NASB). In other words, the *heavens opening* at Jesus's baptism by John was not a simple parting of the clouds. It was a violent act, first represented by Isaiah's language when he prayed *"rend the heavens and come down"* (Isa. 64:1). An invitation had been made on behalf of humanity, and God answered in person.

Tearing the heavens was in itself an act of ultimate grace and glory, resulting in spiritual forces of darkness suffering serious consequences. The Man, Christ Jesus, is now clothed with Heaven, thoroughly equipped for all His earthly purposes. And His equipping was a prophetic foretaste of what would soon be made available to all.

Signs to Make You Wonder

The veil in the temple, the rocks around Jerusalem, and the heavens all experience the same act of violence. They give witness that the King with a superior Kingdom has just come onto the scene.

- *The veil*—God was not tied to an Old Covenant anymore as the requirements had been met through Jesus's death. It was torn top to bottom, as it was His doing.

- *The rocks*—the hardest places on earth were responding to the change in seasons, splitting open to signify that Jesus, the King of glory, was welcome to rule here.

- *The heavens*—the prince of the power of the air had no authority over Jesus, who would be the prototype of every believer who would walk the earth after His death, resurrection, and ascension into Heaven.

So then, what happened when the heavens were torn open in this act of violence? The Spirit of God came down. This is the answer to Isaiah's prayer. This is in response to the cries of the kings and prophets who all ached for this day. Jesus paved the way for His experience to become our experience. The Holy Spirit, the treasure of Heaven that Jesus and the Father spoke so reverently about, has been released on earth. To look for another open Heaven is to incorrectly steward the one we've been given.

OPEN HEAVENS

Every believer has an open Heaven. For the believer, most closed heavens are between the ears. Living as though the heavens were brass over us actually plays into the devil's hands as it puts us in a defensive posture. This violates what Jesus accomplished. He put us on offense with His commission, *"Go!"* Remember, believing a lie empowers the liar.

This certainly doesn't mean that darkness isn't able to cast a long shadow over a person, or even a city or a nation. We often find ourselves in spiritually dark environments. I can take you places where just being there could cause you to tremble, as the realm of darkness is so prevalent, destructive, and dominant. Even so, it is an inferior power, one I cannot afford to be impressed with. My attention must be on the provisions and promises of Christ and the open Heaven over me. I believe that keeping my focus on those things describes at least in part what it means to abide in Christ (see John 15:4). Plus, our refusal to fear reminds the devil that he is finished! (See Philippians 1:28.) If for some reason you can't seem to sense what to do in a given environment, worship. When in doubt, always worship.

We cannot let darkness shape our awareness of the heavenly atmosphere that dwells upon us. The *size* of the open heaven over us is affected in some measure by our maturity and yieldedness to the Holy Spirit. Think of the open Heaven as a big oak tree. The bigger and more stable the tree is, the more people can stand under its shade. Mature believers carry Heaven's atmosphere in such a way that others are able to stand under their shade and receive protection. To use another analogy, others can *draft* on our breakthroughs and become changed.

To live unaware of the open Heaven over us is to contribute to the war over our hearts and minds as it pertains to the truth of Scripture. Then we will always see what hasn't happened instead of living from what has happened. We owe it to God to live aware of what He has done and draw from the reality He has made available. Not doing so costs us dearly. The heavens were torn open, and there is no demonic power that is able to sew them back together. Besides, the Father longs for the Spirit who lives in us. What power of darkness exists that could block their fellowship? But when we live with a primary awareness of the enemy and his plans, we instinctively live in reaction to darkness. Again, if I do, then the enemy has had a role in influencing my agenda. And he isn't worthy. My life must be lived in response to what the Father is doing. That is the life Jesus modeled for us.

Heaven is filled with perfect confidence and peace, while this world is filled with chaos and mistrust in God. We always reflect the nature of the world we are most aware of. Living aware of open heavens has incalculable results.

CAN GOD COME TO WHERE HE IS?

Some are bothered when we talk about God coming into a situation, His Spirit falling upon us, or the Holy Spirit moving in a meeting, etc. Often, as we get ready to minister to people, we will invite the Holy Spirit to come, in the John Wimber fashion. The question is, "Why invite God to come when He is already here?" It's a good question. It makes no sense whatsoever to pray that way unless we understand that there are different measures and dimensions of God's Presence. When He is here, there is always more to come. It's important to hunger for and invite that increase. Isaiah had a perception of this reality, saying, *"I saw the Lord sitting on a throne, lofty and exalted, with the train of His robe filling the temple"* (Isa. 6:1, NASB). The word *filling* implies that His robe filled the temple, but then continued to fill it. He came, but He kept coming. There is always more!

This is at least a partial list of these measures of His Presence; each one is an increase of the previous:

- God first inhabits everything and holds all things together (see Col. 1:17). He is everywhere, the glue that holds His creation in place.

- A second dimension of God's Presence is His indwelling Holy Spirit in the lives of those who have been born again. He specifically comes to make us His tabernacle.

- A third dimension is seen when believers gather in His name. As He promised, He is *"there in their midst"* (Matt. 18:20 NASB). This is where the principle of exponential increase comes into play.

- A fourth measure or dimension occurs when God's people praise Him, for He says He "inhabits the praises of His people" (see Ps. 22:3). He is already in our midst but has chosen to manifest Himself upon us more powerfully in that atmosphere.

- A fifth measure is seen when the Temple of Solomon was dedicated: God came so profoundly that priests were incapacitated (see 1 Kings 8:10-11). No one could even stand, let alone play instruments or sing. They were completely undone at that measure of Presence.

I mention these five levels only as principles, in an effort to give a snapshot of how He longs to increase His manifestation upon His people. The day of Pentecost and the gift of the baptism in the Holy Spirit may in fact illustrate all of these principles combined as an entire city came under the influence of God's manifest Presence.

These various measures of Presence are recorded both in history and in Scripture. Reformation and revival history shows us what's available. The responsibility for the measure of God's Presence that we carry lies with us. We always have what we earnestly want.

LIVING FOR ONE THING

It's easy to get so preoccupied with the vision for our lives that we miss the process entirely. We are here to grow into the maturity of Jesus, bring as many converts to Him as possible, and transform everywhere we have authority and influence. What we sometimes fail to realize is that all of those assignments are impossible. Every one of them. But strangely, they are possible if they are the fruit of something else. And this is *something* we can actually do. Let me explain.

We are called into fellowship with God. In this process, He has made it possible for us not only to come to know Him, but also to have Him live inside of us and even rest upon us. Everything we could ever want out of life flows from that one privilege. King David understood this concept better than most New Testament believers. He referred to it as the *one thing* (see Ps. 27:4). All of life gets reduced to one thing—how we steward the Presence of God. Stewarding the Presence of God, hosting the Presence, is the only way these impossible dreams can be accomplished.

The fulfillment of these dreams is actually the byproduct of hosting Him well. Jesus affirmed this principle for life when He taught, *"But seek first His kingdom and His righteousness, and all these things will be added to you"* (Matt. 6:33, NASB). The Kingdom of God is not something separate from His actual Presence. The Kingdom has a King. In reality, the Kingdom of God is within the Presence of the Spirit of God. *"For the kingdom of God is...in the Holy Spirit"* (Rom. 14:17). This command by Jesus is to prioritize our lives down to the *one thing* which is eventually evidenced by righteous living.

I once had the Lord wake me in the night with His voice. He said that He watches over the watch of those who watch the Lord. It's been a number of years since that encounter. Thinking of that moment still excites and yet puzzles me all at the same time. The "watch" represents God-given responsibilities. It's what a watchman does—he looks over his responsibility to make sure things are safe and properly taken care of. God was essentially telling me that He would watch over my watch (responsibilities) if I would make "watching Him" my only responsibility. It was His invitation for me to become Presence-centered.

When we discuss our responsibilities in life, many good things come to our minds. But for me now it always boils down to the one thing—His Presence. What do I do with His Presence? What place does the manifest Presence of God have with how I think and live? Does the Presence of God affect the vision and focus of my life? What is the impact of the *one thing* on my behavior?

THE GATE TO A TRANSFORMED CITY

In Acts chapter one, Jesus appeared to five hundred people, telling them not to leave Jerusalem until they received the promise of the Father. The remaining eleven disciples of Jesus were a part of this group. The eleven had already received the Holy Spirit in John 20, but were still commanded to stay in Jerusalem for what the Father had promised. A prayer meeting was formed. After ten days, only one hundred and twenty people were left.

As highly regarded as this day is in our hearts, I'm not sure we really see the significance. On the day of Pentecost, the baptism in the Holy Spirit was given. This baptism in the Holy Spirit is called the Father's Promise. The Father, the One who only gives good gifts, has given us this gift. All life flows only from Him. He is the One who is the orchestrator and conductor of life, and He has given a promise. And this is it. This is His special gift. It's a promise that reintroduces us to the original purpose for humanity—a people suited to carry the fullness of God on earth (see Eph. 3:19). This is only possible through the baptism in the Holy Spirit—a baptism of fire!

> *And suddenly **there came from heaven** a noise like a violent rushing wind, and it filled the whole house where they were sitting* (Acts 2:2, NASB).

A noise came from Heaven. Two worlds met. It was like a violent rushing wind. The word *rushing* is *phero*. Out of the sixty-seven times that word is translated in the New Testament, it is *rushing* only once. The other times it has the meaning *to carry*, *to bear*, or *to bring forth*. It would be foolish for me to suggest changing how it's translated. But I would like to suggest adding the *bring forth* aspect to our understanding of its meaning. So then, could the word *rushing* imply that this was a noise, a violent wind, that *carried* or *brought forth* something from its place of origin to its destiny—from Heaven to earth? I think so.

Noise can be translated *roar*. God spoke the worlds into being. His Word is the creative force. *"By the word of the Lord the heavens were made, and by the breath of His mouth all their host"* (Ps. 33:6; see Gen. 1:3-24). This sound could have come from the mouth of God releasing something on the earth that the prophets longed to see and be a part of from the beginning. Add to this the fact that God Himself rides on the wind (see Ps. 104:3). We then see that this is a moment when God, riding on wind, a sound, Heaven's breath, is restoring humankind to purpose. Without question, the most dramatic invasion of Heaven to earth happened in this moment. It was *the* defining moment. This is what the Father promised.

THE AIRWAVES CARRY HEAVEN'S SOUND

This sound did in fact carry a reality from that world into this one. This heavenly sound transformed the atmosphere over the city of Jerusalem. In one moment it was changed from the city that crucified Jesus to a city that wanted to know what to do to be saved. How did that happen? Through sound—a sound from Heaven. Both sound and light are vibrations. And on this day it was the vibration of Heaven that introduced a different drumbeat to a city that was unaware of whose drumbeat they were marching to. For the first time they could see.

The house of God is the gate of Heaven. Remember, it's the house built on the edge of two worlds. And right here we see the effect on its surroundings when they became open to what God is doing. There was a literal release of something from that world, *through the gate* into this one. And a city was positioned to experience unfathomable change.

The heavenly sound was heard and experienced on earth. The roar of Heaven summoned this city to its purpose and call. In this moment, two worlds collided, and the inferior realm of darkness gave way to the superior nature of His Kingdom. We have the unique privilege of carrying His Presence. In doing so, we cause this kind of conflict so that these two realities, called Heaven and earth, could dance together in perfect harmony.

This picture is similar to the picture given at Jesus's baptism in that it was a violent activity from Heaven. It upset the powers that were accustomed to occupying that space. And in Acts 2, the Holy Spirit was released in the same way as at Jesus's baptism—this time upon His people instead of upon Jesus. It's important to note that violence in the spiritual realm is always a peace-filled moment for His people. That's how the Prince of Peace can crush satan under our feet (see Rom. 16:20). Another way to put it is every peace-filled moment you experience brings terror to the powers of darkness. Only in the Kingdom of God is peace a military tool.

A City Restored

When that mysterious sound was released at Pentecost, thousands of people began to gather to the one hundred and twenty at the upper room. It was nine o'clock in the morning. People were still preparing for the day. But they dropped everything. Men laid down their tools, women had their children put down their toys. A sound filled the air that also filled their hearts. Imagine an atmospheric shift over an entire city.

This is the city that rose up to crucify Jesus. His Presence among them was the one good thing they had, and they destroyed it by responding to the spirit of murder, the one thing civilized people pride themselves on resisting. Yet what erupted out of the heart of God, the sound that was released through that open Heaven, erupted over an entire city. No one knows why the crowd gathered in front of the upper room. No handbills or posters were distributed. No announcements were made. But a sound was released over them that cleared the air for the first time in their lives. Their thoughts were clear. They could reason. They sensed divine purpose. It seemed as though God was summoning people. And that's exactly what happened.

Growing up, I always thought people gathered because the one hundred and twenty were speaking in tongues, which was in the people's native languages. But that doesn't make sense, especially for an international city where foreign visitors are common. They gathered to a sound, an indistinguishable sound, one that reached deep into the hearts of people. Apart from an act of God, it would be nearly impossible to cause people to leave their businesses, homes, and activity centers to gather for no known reason. This sound called to something deep within the heart of this city, calling to restore it to its original purpose. This city was to be known as a city of His Presence. King David made that dedication so many years earlier in the tabernacle he built within that city which was dedicated to 24/7 worship.

To illustrate the nature of this sound, I like to compare it to that of a musical instrument. A gifted musician can get an almost magical sound out of the saxophone as they skillfully breathe across the reed properly placed in the mouthpiece of the instrument. Now in the same way, consider the breath of God blowing across the reed of the hearts of one hundred and twenty people releasing a sound over a city that changed its atmosphere. When you change an atmosphere, you change a destiny. That's what people heard. A *harmonic* sound that came because one hundred and twenty were together in *unity*, not only with each other, but with the Spirit of the resurrected Christ. That is the sound that was heard some 2,000 years ago. It was a sound that initiated the ushering in of 3,000 people in one day. A momentum was created through this open Heaven that made it so people were *added* to their numbers daily (see Acts 2:47). That continued until it opened even more and they moved from *addition* to *multiplication* (see Acts 9:31).

ONCE A COWARD, NOT ALWAYS A COWARD

When Peter saw the crowds gather, he had an uncontrollable urge to preach. This man, who was a coward only days ago when questioned by a servant girl (see Mark 14:69), now stood heroically before thousands to proclaim the good news. Remember, it wasn't just the fact that he had to give witness to a large crowd. It was before a crowd that was now mocking what they saw once they were drawn to that place. This sermon came in the midst of the most unusual manifestations by God's chosen people. The crowd thought the hundred and twenty people were drunk. But often what we think drives the world away from the Gospel actually brings them to it. It only drives away those who have been taught against it. (Many think God's reputation is somehow protected when our dignity is preserved. And yet God is constantly asking us to lay down our rights—even to dignity.) Courage rose up in Peter's heart, and he made sense of it all and brought forth the perfect message for this moment. Cowards are only *one touch from God* away from becoming courageous preachers with great power.

"What must we do to be saved?" (See Acts 2:37.) That's quite a response from the people who crucified Jesus only weeks earlier. Was it Peter's sermon? While I don't want to take away from the moment of profound bravery, Peter preached under an open Heaven. This atmosphere carried the sound of Heaven that changed the mindsets of an entire city in moments. His message was quite brief. But it was filled with power, and it brought understanding so that the nervous mockery stopped and the real issues of the heart could be seen. In this one message, 3,000 people were saved. This becomes the devil's worst possible nightmare. Suddenly, things progressed from the anointing/open Heaven existing over one Man, Jesus, to the one hundred and twenty, and now imparted to 3,000 new believers. The potential of this movement is unlimited, until the whole earth is filled with His glory! And that is God's intention through those who host Him well, all while yielding to the wonderful Holy Spirit.

WHAT IT'S ALL ABOUT

I have a Pentecostal background, for which I am very thankful. My forefathers paid quite a price to preach and defend that the baptism in the Spirit and speaking in tongues is still for today. I owe it to them to do nothing to take away from their accomplishments, but to add all I can. Having said that, I have seen that many have come to the wrong conclusions about this Holy Spirit baptism. It's not for tongues (which I believe is important and available to *everyone*). It's for *power*. And it's not just power for miracles. It's so that the power-charged atmosphere of Heaven can rest upon a person, which forces a shift in the atmosphere over a home, business, or city. This baptism is to make us living witnesses and examples of the resurrection of Jesus—the ultimate display of Heaven's power. The Spirit of the resurrected Christ is what filled the air on the day of Pentecost.

The Long Prayer Meeting

I can only imagine that after ten days of praying together they were tired and had probably exhausted everything they could think of to pray about. Suddenly, their affection for Jesus was taken to a level they had never known or experienced before. Their spirits became empowered by the Holy Spirit in that *suddenly* moment. They were alive, really alive for the first time in their lives. They spoke of things they didn't understand. Two worlds collided. And the understanding of God that exists in that heavenly realm actually influenced the language of the one hundred and twenty here on earth. They spoke of the mysterious ways and the mighty deeds of God.

This baptism is likened to *wine* and not *water*. Water refreshes while wine influences. When God calls a particular baptism a *baptism of fire*, it is obviously not one of mere refreshing. Heaven has come to influence earth in this baptism. But when that rushing mighty wind came and the language of Heaven poured forth from their lips, they also were refreshed by what influenced them. Paul would later point out that praying in tongues edifies us. There's little doubt about that happening to this small group. To top it off, they were speaking something so completely satisfying, so accurate and powerful, that it was like experiencing a completely new day. And they were. This heavenly language came as an eruption from their hearts. But for the first time in their lives, and actually in all of history, they said what needed to be said perfectly without missing it or falling short in one way or another.

The Spirit of God spoke through them with brilliant understanding of whom He was exalting. Their praise went right from the Spirit of God, through their yielded lips, to God Himself. In this instance, the human intellect was bypassed. They were *"speaking of the mighty deeds of God"* (Acts 2:11, NASB). This time, the language was a language of praise—not prayer. Imagine the privilege it was to speak of the great mysteries of God's nature over a city that had rejected Him. It was intoxicating, to say the least. The intention of the Lord is that this baptism of fire would ignite every heart. This would be best expressed by a people who were Presence-driven instead of ministry-driven. It's not about what I can accomplish for God. It's all about who goes with me and my doing all I can to protect that most valuable connection.

WHEN MORE LEADS TO MORE

A few years after this great outpouring of the Spirit, things were still going quite well. In fact, the numbers were increasing daily, and miracles would shake an entire city. Peter and John released a miracle to a lame man that seemed to shake up everyone (see Acts 3:1-10). They were credited as having great boldness. As a result, they were arrested, interrogated, persecuted, and finally released. Upon their release they went to a prayer meeting and prayed for more boldness.

> *And now, Lord, take note of their threats, and grant that Your bond-servants may speak Your word with all confidence, while You extend Your hand to heal, and signs and wonders take place through the name of Your holy servant Jesus* (Acts 4:29-30, NASB).

And the Spirit of God came in again. We always need more.

Many who speak in tongues think they are full of the Holy Spirit. Being full of Holy Spirit is not evidenced in tongues; it is evidenced by being full. How do you know when a glass is completely full? It runs over. Peter, on the day of Pentecost, is filled with Holy Spirit. In Acts 4, Peter joins many others in a prayer meeting. Their overwhelming expression was to cry out for more. Peter prayed for more. He did not pray for relief in the midst of persecution, but instead for more boldness, that expression that sometimes offends, so that he could go deeper into the realms of darkness and pull out more victims. And the Bible says:

> *And when they had prayed, the place where they had gathered together was shaken, and they were all filled with the Holy Spirit and began to speak the word of God with boldness* (Acts 4:31, NASB).

In Acts 2, Peter is filled. In Acts 4, he needs to be refilled. Why? If you are doing this right, you must get filled often. There is one baptism. But we are to live in such a way that we give away all we get, while our capacity for Him increases. When we live full of the Holy Spirit, experiencing overflow, only more of Him will do. Needing to be refilled is not a sign of something gone wrong. Continual dependence on *more* is a good thing.

Purpose of Outpouring

It is so easy to assume that something like the baptism in the Holy Spirit is primarily to make us more useful in ministry. That makes us *top heavy* in the sense that we become *professionals* in areas of life that were really reserved for *romantics*. My friend Bob Kilpatrick would call that approach *law* instead of *art*.[1] There are parts of our walk with Christ that should never be reduced to a list of goals and accomplishments. Instead, this unimaginable privilege of carrying His Presence should never reduce me to a laborer for God. The decision of being a servant or a friend is still being chosen by people around us every day. While it is one of my highest privileges to serve Him completely, my labor is the byproduct of my love. This baptism introduces us to intimacy at the highest possible level.

The heart of God in this matter is clearly seen in this amazing prophecy from Ezekiel. *"I will not hide my face from them any longer, for I will have poured out my Spirit"* (Ezek. 39:29, NASB). In the outpouring of the Holy Spirit is the revelation of the face of God. There is nothing greater. *"In the light of the king's face is life, and his favor is like a cloud with the spring rain"* (Prov. 16:15, NASB). Rain is a biblical metaphor for the move of the Holy Spirit, thus the term *outpouring*. This verse also links God's face, His favor, with the outpouring of His Spirit.[2]

The revelation of the face of God through the outpouring of the Spirit is made available to everyone. The outpouring in Acts 2 was the beginning. The outpouring of the Spirit is the fulfillment of the quest for God's face. This means that wherever we go in revival, we can't go past the face. The only direction to go is to cry out for a greater measure of His Presence in the outpouring. Psalm 80 links the favor of His face with the work of His hand. The righteous who seek His face in intimacy are those who can be used to do great exploits. Heroes of the faith became men and women *"of* [God's] *right hand"* (Ps. 80:17). He put them on like a glove and used them to display His signs and wonders. We must be those who see what's available and contend for a greater measure of His favor to be upon us.

Moses experienced the transforming Presence on his own face. It was the result of his own face-to-face encounter with God. The outpouring brings us to His face again. And believe it or not, Moses's experience pales by comparison. *"How will the ministry of the Spirit fail to be even more with glory?"* (2 Cor. 3:8, NASB). So then, as we prioritize hosting His Presence, we learn to release His face of favor into the earth. That is what people of great favor do.

Endnotes

1. *The Art of Being You: How to Live as God's Masterpiece* by Bob and Joel Kilpatrick tackles this issue beautifully. It is from Zondervan Publishing.

2. Bill Johnson's book, *Face to Face with God*, from Charisma Publishing takes this theme as its primary focus.

SEND THE RAIN!

It's one thing to preach about the glory of God; it is another dimension entirely to experience it firsthand. When the reality of an open heaven starts to translate from what we preach about on Sunday morning or read about in our Bible study time, to becoming something that we see, taste, and experience with our senses, we are starting to walk in what God made available.

Scripture has not been given to us simply to read with our coffee in the mornings, or preach from a pulpit one or twice a week. The Bible is a divine summons into encounter. Everything we read about in Scripture invites us to see what's on the page released into everyday life. The key to seeing Scripture transition from written word to demonstrated reality is the relentless, desperate cry, "God, there must be more!"

When Pastor John Kilpatrick shares about the season leading up to the Brownsville Revival (1995-2000), his testimony is filled with the language of holy discontentment. Throughout his ministry, he had experienced light showers of rain. He saw people saved, healed, and baptized in the Holy Spirit. These are certainly glorious experiences to celebrate. At the same time, Kilpatrick yearned for more. Even though he had a growing church, a successful television ministry, and a blessed family life, he found himself gripped—overwhelmed—by the conviction that there was more. He grew tired preaching about realities that he and his church community were experiencing.

This cry for God's glory set Pastor John Kilpatrick on a journey that would lead to the Brownsville Revival... but not culminate with it. Even though Brownsville is considered by many to be one of the longest sustained revival movements in the United Stated, with millions being impacted by its fruit, Kilpatrick never settled into a Christianity of contentment. He kept pressing onward. As a result, he experienced a second blessing when the Bay of the Holy Spirit Revival broke out at Church of His Presence in Daphne, AL. This season of visitation was accompanied by supernatural manifestations of healings, signs and wonders. And yet, Kilpatrick still cries out for more.

To this day, Pastor John Kilpatrick longs for an increase of revival among the people of God. His desperate cry is for the body of Christ to live as a habitation for the Holy Spirit, not simply be content with "church as usual."

The following is adapted from one of his contributing chapters in the book, *The Fire that Never Sleeps.*

CHAPTER 5

THE CRY FOR GOD'S GLORY

John Kilpatrick

All revival begins, and continues, in the prayer meeting.
—HENRY BLACKABY

I have learned that revival is definitely *not* church as usual. "Usual" represents what we have become accustomed to—our concept of normal Christianity. When revival comes, everything changes. Normal becomes radically redefined. This is exactly what we must be pressing in for in the place of prayer. Revival is not optional for the desperate person; it is the *only option*.

REVIVAL IS AN OVER-ANSWER TO PRAYER

I like to call revival an *over*-answer to prayer. We cry out for one thing, having some vague idea of what we think the answer should look like. Remember, revival is completely supernatural. God sends it, and anything sent from God's realm carries His DNA. Paul reminds us that we serve the One who "is able to do far more abundantly beyond all that we ask or think, according to the power that works within us" (Eph. 3:20, NASB).

What takes place during revival is, without a doubt, outside the parameters of normal Christianity, as defined by modern religious culture. It's not church as usual because the magnitude of God's Presence is infinitely greater than it is during average, normal church. *Presence* is the key distinguishing factor of revival, which we will explore in greater detail later in this chapter. For now, it is important to recognize that revival is qualified because of how God's weighty, glorious Presence crashes in on a place and a people. This is where we experience the *over*-answer to prayer. When God comes with His manifest Presence, our experience is far beyond our greatest expectations.

Even though revival is an over-answer to prayer, it is still an answer to *prayer*. In the years leading up to the Brownsville Revival, the Lord lead me to establish a house of prayer in our church. By August 1992, and throughout that September, I decided that instead of preaching at our Sunday night services, I would pray for anyone who wanted to receive the baptism of the Holy Spirit. That first night, over one hundred people came forward to receive the baptism, and many more came forward for specific prayer. This was my first major decision to do church *unusually*. I exchanged the typical Sunday night teaching time for prayer. The next Sunday night was equally as powerful. The momentum was growing and there was no way I could back down now. The Holy Spirit made it clear to me that prayer was a priority we were neglecting. Our services focused on everything else—worship, the offering, preaching—but prayer has been reduced to a little bit of altar time when we prayed with the people.

In order to accommodate revival, we need to be willing to move beyond the comfortable and familiar. The Holy Spirit wants to move in every single church community in the world. This is a fact. The reason He does not is because many of these communities are unwilling to host Him and cater to His preferences. My decision to integrate Sunday night prayer meetings into the culture at Brownsville was monumental in preparing us for revival. This was not a John Kilpatrick decision; it was a Holy Spirit directive. He told me, "If you will return to the God of your childhood—if you will make this a house of prayer—I will pour out my Spirit here." Without His instruction, I might have continued on, stuck in the same old rut, doing what we always did and seeing what we always saw.

The truth is, *there is no quick and easy way to revival.* We are not going to have true, lasting revival without prayer. This is why God placed me with Brother Wetzel all those years ago. He mentored me in the very thing that was catalytic to revival: *prayer.* Not casual prayer. Not convenient prayer. Not common prayer. *Nothing about revival is birthed in common places. If we desire to see God move in extraordinary ways, we must be willing to do some extraordinary things.* If you want to experience the *over*-answer of revival, you must be willing to dedicate yourself to the place of prayer. Not in a religious, ritualistic way.

The reason we are going on this journey together is to give you a vision for what prayer accomplishes. When someone tells us, "Pray because God says so" or "Pray because that is what you should do as a Christian," there is little motivation to do it. We need a clear vision of what prayer can produce in our lives, in our churches, in our families, in our cities, and, yes, even in our nations. When we see what's on the other side of prayer, it is no longer a burden or chore; it is our great and high privilege as believers. To think, the great God has extended an invitation for you and me to partner with Him *through prayer.*

I had no idea how prayer would position Brownsville to become a place of divine visitation. To this day, I remain humbled and awestruck at God's choice to make our little community in Pensacola a place where the Holy Spirit touched the masses and multitudes were launched into global mission efforts. All I know is that prayer is an essential forerunner to revival; I learned this through personal experience.

REVIVAL IS WHEN THE GLORY COMES

One simple way to determine whether you are experiencing revival is by answering the question: Is God's glory there? Unfortunately the word *glory* has become lost in a sea of Christian jargon. As a result we really don't know what it means anymore. When we don't know what it means, we don't have a vision for it. And when we don't have a vision for God's glory saturating our homes, churches, and communities, we will not cry out for it with great desperation. Divine visitation is marked by the unmistakable Presence of God's glory.

In order to clearly define *glory*, we need to make the important distinction between two seemingly related topics: anointing and glory.

The Anointing

The anointing is the supernatural endowment of the Holy Spirit upon a person's life to do the works of the ministry. You could also see it as a divine authorization to operate in the grace and power of the Spirit in your life.

In Luke 4:18 (NKJV), we see Jesus introduce His public ministry with these words:

> *The Spirit of the Lord is upon Me, Because He has anointed Me...*

Jesus continues to explain *what* He was anointed to *do*:

> *To preach the gospel to the poor; He has sent Me to heal the brokenhearted, To proclaim liberty to the captives And recovery of sight to the blind, To set at liberty those who are oppressed; To proclaim the acceptable year of the Lord* (Luke 4:18-19, NKJV).

The anointing has been made available to every single Christian, since every true born-again person has received the Holy Spirit (see 1 Cor. 3:16, 6:19). Be that as it may, not every believer draws from this endless well of supernatural supply and power. It is readily available. The question is, are you accessing everything that is available?

If you have the Holy Spirit living inside you, you have been anointed to do the works of ministry. God's Presence empowers you to do what you could not accomplish with your natural strength and ability. The anointing gives you supernatural wisdom and understanding. The anointing makes you conscious of the Spirit's Presence with you and in you. The anointing gives preachers unction to preach, evangelists grace to proclaim the Gospel message, prophets the ability to prophesy, teachers the articulation to communicate truth, and pastors the compassion to shepherd. The anointing gives you business strategy, creative ideas, and decision-making clarity.

The anointing of the Holy Spirit is His supernatural Presence within you to do what you could not do with your natural human ability. It really is Heaven's authorization upon you to do the works of Jesus *on earth*—in whatever sphere of influence you have been called to.

The Glory

The glory is *not* the anointing—the glory is the manifest Presence of God. *This* is the over-answer to prayer that I described earlier in this chapter. Even though all Christians are filled with the Holy Spirit, there is another dimension of experiencing His Presence. It is this unusual expression of God's manifest Presence that sets revival apart from church as usual.

Even people who are not anointed can feel and experience the Presence of God's glory. This is common during revival. In fact, I saw it firsthand at Brownsville as those who were far away from God ran toward the altar night after night. Why? Deep conviction of sin? Yes. But what brought about this conviction of sin? Outside those doors, people thought everything was okay. Sin was tolerable in their lives. Immorality was acceptable. Addiction was usual. They did not become convicted of sin just going through the motions of their everyday lives. Rather, they *did* experience deep conviction of sin in an environment saturated with the glory of God.

This does not have to take place in a building or a church. Revival history is full of examples where the glory of God refused to be contained by a building. The preaching of Methodist founder John Wesley and evangelist George Whitefield did not win converts because of high eloquence or stunning oration. Although these men were both anointed individuals, there was an unusual measure of glory in their preaching. They could truly echo the words of Paul, who wrote,

> *And I, when I came to you, brothers, did not come proclaiming to you the testimony of God with lofty speech or wisdom.* For I decided to know nothing among you except Jesus Christ and him crucified. And I was with you in weakness and in fear and much trembling, and my speech and my message were not in plausible words of wisdom, but in demonstration of the Spirit and of power, so that your faith might not rest in the wisdom of men but in the power of God (1 Corinthians 2:1-5).

Paul's preaching carried the manifest Presence of God. In the same manner, Great Awakening revivalists like Wesley, Whitefield, Charles Finney, and Jonathan Edwards preached and God's glory was released.

The people exposed to such preaching did not simply make intellectual decisions to follow Jesus; many were so deeply touched that their physical bodies reacted in various ways to the glory of God that was present *upon* the preaching. It was said that people were encouraged *not* to listen to the evangelists while sitting up in trees, in fear that the weight of God's glory would knock them right out of the branches.

In the Old Testament, the Hebrew word for *glory* is *kabowd*. One of the first places this word is mentioned is Exodus 16:10 (KJV):

> *And it came to pass, as Aaron spake unto the whole congregation of the children of Israel, that they looked toward the wilderness, and, behold, the glory of the Lord appeared in the cloud.*

What the congregation of Israel saw was the manifest, visible Presence of the Lord. It was not conceptual. It was not spiritual language used to describe a feeling, expression, or an act of thanksgiving toward God. When the glory came in the Old Testament, the atmosphere changed. The people stood awestruck, often in helpless wonder. Priests could not continue to minister under its weight.

The glory is that weighty Presence of God that can blanket an entire gathering—or even a community. Read the powerful testimonies from the first Great Awakening in New England or the Welsh Revival of 1904, and you will see entire communities under that weighty canopy of God's manifest Presence. This is what I long for, and it is what I have given my ministry to protecting.

As pastors and leaders, we are custodians of God's Presence. It is all about doing everything to make the Holy Spirit comfortable in our midst. When all is said and done, there is only so much that we can offer people. Whether you are in the ministry or not, there is only so much you can give those who are hurting and hopeless. When we encounter God's glory, we are exposed to the great solution to humankind's state. Identity is found in the glory. Healing comes in the glory. True purpose and meaning are discovered in the glory. Humanity lives blind to these realities because of its sinful condition. What is the condition? The human race became infected with sin because of the exchange in the Garden of Eden.

RESTORED TO THE GLORY

One of the most significant things about sin is that it broke humankind away from its original position—living in the glory. The glory is both God's standard and God's manifest Presence. Sometimes we read familiar Scripture passages like, "for all have sinned and fall short of the glory of God" (Rom. 3:23, NKJV), and maintain a limited perspective of their complete meaning. When Adam sinned, he fell short of God's holy standard, most certainly. But he also surrendered his adornment of glory.

David mentions this garment in Psalm 8:5 as he reflects upon God's interaction with humankind, His great creation: "Yet you have made him a little lower than the heavenly beings and crowned him with glory and honor."

The same Hebrew word that describes the weighty, visible, manifest Presence of God—*kabowd*—is used in Psalm 8:5 to express the measure of glory that humankind enjoyed in the early days of creation. *We were uniquely fashioned to live in God's glory.* In Eden, Adam and Eve were naked. They were always naked, but when they sinned the glory lifted and they realized they were naked. In turn, they started reaching in their own ability—trying to cover up their shame. Humankind has been trying to cover its spiritual nakedness ever since Eden. The only solution is the blood of Jesus.

Spiritually contaminated by sin, Adam could no longer continue wearing a garment of glory. Sin made him incompatible with this state of perfection, and thus he fell short of living *clothed* in God's glory. In Romans 3:23, glory comes from the Greek word *doxa*, which refers to splendor, brightness, and kindly majesty. These words describe the Presence of the King of Glory. Everything that describes who God is emanates from His being. His very nature *creates* a Presence. In the same way that certain character traits seem to create an atmosphere around some people, be it good or bad, the same thing is true of God. We prefer to be around those whose personalities create a positive atmosphere of joy, peace, encouragement, and kindness. Consider what kind of atmosphere the nature of God creates around Him. Adam lived in this, but then fell beneath it because of sin.

This is why the Gospel is such good news on boundless levels. *Because of Jesus's atoning blood, you have become compatible again with the garments of God's glory.* This is why revival does not destroy people today. Even those who don't know God can taste a measure of His glory in the atmosphere of revival. In fact, the touch of God's glory is often what draws lost people to repentance and the prodigals to renewed devotion to Christ.

REVIVAL IS MARKED BY THE PRESENCE OF GOD'S GLORY

Revival happens when you can feel the weighty atmosphere of God's Presence to the point that it becomes therapeutic. Duncan Campbell defined this measure of glory as a "community saturated with God."

Countless testimonies have been shared by those who experienced healing or deliverance simply by being *in* the glory of God's Presence. No one laid hands on them. No one even prayed for them. God's glory just came upon these people and released such a therapeutic touch that if you were emotionally unstable or mentally tormented, it calmed you immediately. If you suffered a physical condition, that glorious Presence would release healing. In revival, the Presence of God's glory creates dynamic, measurable transformation in people. Perhaps one of the most common evidences of God's glory in our midst is the frequency with which people are struck with conviction.

During "church as usual," we may experience a limited measure of God's Presence. It is only when revival permeates the atmosphere that there is an unprecedented outpouring of God's weighty glory. It is only as we experience this measure of God's Presence that we discover what revival *truly is*.

I have traveled many places, and I cannot tell you how many times people have told me, "Brother Kilpatrick, I can't believe you are here! We're believing God for a revival." When you start looking beneath the surface, what these people are expecting and pursuing is not revival at all. They want crowds, recognition, fame, a Presence on Christian TV, and media. For the heart that is sincerely desperate to encounter God's Presence, revival is not an add-on to everything else we have embraced as Christian living. Revival is about rejecting the false and embracing the authentic. Revival draws a clear line in the sand. It gets messy and is often controversial. People are given the option to continue to embrace what the Holy Spirit is doing, on His terms, or go back to "normal." For the man or woman contending for revival, there is simply *no* normal to go back to.

This is when you know that a community is sincerely hungry for true revival. We don't pursue revival as an *addition* to what we are already doing as believers or leaders. Our quest for revival is motivated by a desire to exchange our ways for God's way. We pursue revival because we are tired of going through religious motions. A measure of success does not satisfy us. Popularity pales in comparison to enjoying the nearness of God's Presence. A good job, a happy family, and a casual relationship with Jesus do not bring deep fulfillment.

What is the deep cry of the hungry and thirsty soul?

> *One thing have I asked of the Lord, that will I seek after: that I may dwell in the house of the Lord all the days of my life, to gaze upon the beauty of the Lord and to inquire in his temple* (Psalm 27:4).

> *How lovely is your dwelling place, O Lord of hosts! My soul longs, yes, faints for the courts of the Lord; my heart and flesh sing for joy to the living God* (Psalm 84:1-2).

As the deer longs for streams of water, so I long for you,
O God. I thirst for God, the living God. When can I go
and stand before him? (Psalm 42:1-2, NLT)

Our desperate cry is for God's glorious Presence. *This* is the measuring stick of revival. We might conduct prolonged church services, hold meetings, and orchestrate events, but if there is no hunger for and encounter with the glory of God, we are continuing to do church as usual.

I don't know about you, but I'm tired of the usual.

Rev. Tommy Tenney was a prophetic voice and forerunner for the present revival movement. During a season when Christianity had become very much principle-driven, Tenney boldly summoned the body of Christ back to the sacred place of God's Presence.

God Chasers was not merely a book that was written; it was a message that was experienced in the trenches and then translated to paper. To this day, when the title is mentioned, many remember exactly where they were when that urgent message graced their lives and helped force them out of the rut of "Christianity as usual" and onto a relentless quest to experience the same manifest Presence of God that Tenney did. After all, God is no respecter of persons. If He could be chased... and caught... by Tommy Tenney, He can likewise be caught by you.

The entire work of *God Chasers* is just as significant today, if not more so, than it was upon initial publication. The positive fruit is that there are multitudes of believers across the earth today who are intentionally pursuing God's Presence like never before. They are not content with information about God; they want to know Him personally. They aren't just after the healings, breakthroughs and answered prayers; they actually delight in the breakthroughs because they give visible expression to the very nature of an invisible God. Tenney sowed seeds through *God Chasers* that are still producing harvest.

At the same time, Tenney himself would tell you not to settle for the present measure of outpouring. With God, there is always more and messages like *God Chasers* are intended to keep you hungry. Sustained hunger and thirst for God are what we need in the church today. It's not enough to have been around during the revival movements of the 1990's, or to have had a powerful experience with God at a meeting, church service, or conference. Yesterday is worth celebrating, but we cannot live there. It's not enough to have tasted...and then camped out at that one taste, or worse, experienced a taste of Heaven and then went back to the old normal. Every time you catch Him, you are being ushered into a new normal.

To stagnate in our quest for God is to believe a lie. That is what it ultimately comes down to. We cannot cease or lose momentum, as we have yet to see entire cities saved and regions transformed. We have yet to hear of meetings where every single sick body is miraculously cured. We have yet to hear of morgues being emptied out, as the dead are being raised on a regular basis. Certainly, there are some who would consider these words "pie in the sky" Christianity. I cannot. You cannot. We cannot rest until we see the very miracles and works of Jesus, both repeated and exceeded. Yes exceeded, as this is the very lifestyle He invited you and I into in John 14:12.

The following is a chapter from Tommy Tenney's classic book, *The God Chasers*.

CHAPTER 6

HE'S DONE IT BEFORE; HE CAN DO IT AGAIN

Tommy Tenney

Send the rain, Lord!

We want God to change the world. But He cannot change the world until He can change us. In our present state we are in no position to affect anything. But if we will submit to the Master Potter, He will make us—all of us—into what He needs us to be. He may remake the vessel of our flesh many times, but if we will submit to the Potter's touch, He can turn us into vessels of honor, power, and life. After all, wasn't He the One who turned unlearned fishermen into world-changers and hated tax collectors into fearless revivalists? If He did it once, He can do it again!

I want to break the standard writing "rules" for Christian books and ask you to pray a prayer with me right now, as you read the first page of this chapter. This compilation was written to help usher God's

Presence into your life and church family. It may sound silly, but I want you to put your hand on your heart and pray this "prayer of the clay" with me right now:

> *Father, we thank You for Your Presence.*
> *Lord, the air is just pregnant with possibility and we sense Your nearness.*
> *But we must say that You are not near enough.*
> *Come, Holy Spirit. If not now, when? If not us, who? And if not here, where?*
> *Just tell us, Lord, and we'll go; we will pursue Your Presence because we want You, Lord.*
> *Your Presence is what we are after and nothing less will do.*

Something is happening in the body of Christ. More and more of us are unwilling to play the old religious games. Something like a warrior spirit is rising up within us, an urge to conquer territory in the name of the Eternal One. I know that in my life, I've received a mandate from the Lord to pour my life into key cities where I sense God intends to pour out His Spirit in the days ahead.

I'm shopping for places where God is "breaking out." Early on in *God Chasers,* I described how God "broke out" in the city of Houston (and I mention it simply because I was privileged to be present when God came on the scene). I have felt led to participate in continual meetings for more than a year in some places, and incredible things are happening. We still have a long way to go, but in each city we did something that has deep spiritual significance for this move of God. I want to see a contagious outbreak of God like was seen with Finney, Edwards, Roberts, and company, where whole regions are swept into the Kingdom.

I'm After Entire Cities

I am after cities; I'm not interested in just preaching in churches to Christian people. I'm after entire cities occupied by people who don't know Jesus. Once while preaching at a conference with Frank Damazio in Portland, Oregon, I heard him mention something that instantly captured my attention. He said that a number of pastors in the Portland area had united together to drive some stakes in the ground at strategic places around the perimeter of their region and the city and at every major intersection. The process took them hours because they also prayed over those stakes, as they were physical symbols marking a spiritual declaration and demarcation line.

I felt the stirring of the Holy Spirit so I said, "Frank, if you'll provide the stakes, then I will go to cities I feel called to and help the pastors stake out that territory for God." Then I began to ask God in prayer, "Lord, give me some precedent so I can understand what You are doing here. Then I'll know why You have pressed this into my heart." Ironically, this stirring of the Lord came upon me later in California, and I was reminded that California was the site of the great "gold rush." Whenever would-be gold prospectors found a spot of ground where they thought there might be some gold, they would "stake a claim." Some plots of property are just more valuable than others because of what is in the ground. If you wanted to claim a plot of ground in those days, then you would "stake" it by driving a stake into the earth. That stake would bear your name and a rough description of the area you were claiming. Later the land would be formally surveyed, but until then, a claim stake was as good as a land deed in a court of law back in those days. If anybody disputed your claim, you could go to that undisturbed plot of ground and dig up your stake bearing your name and the rough dimensions of the claim and say, "See, I've claimed it according to law. I am in the process of possession and occupation, but this claim stake is proof that the land is already mine by law."

Pastors and congregations who have put down roots in a city or region have a "legal right" under God to claim their cities for the King by "staking" out the territory. In the past, too many of us have been content to keep our faith contained within the four walls of our meeting halls and church buildings. Now God is calling us to extend our faith beyond to the boundaries of our cities and nation. In effect, we are literally expanding the "walls" of our spiritual churches when we stake out our cities. It forces us to see ourselves as "the Church" in the city, one people under God comprised of many congregations according to the first century pattern of the "city-church."

We actually made wooden stakes with four sides bearing the words, "Renewal, Revival, Reconciliation," along with supporting Scriptures. A hole was drilled down the middle of the stake and a rolled-up written proclamation was inserted in it. Altogether, there are about twenty Bible verses in the stakes and proclamation, but one of them is Isaiah 62, which says:

> *Behold, the Lord hath proclaimed unto the end of the world, Say ye to the daughter of Zion, Behold, thy salvation cometh; behold, His reward is with Him, and His work before Him. And they shall call them, The holy people, The redeemed of the Lord: and thou shalt be called, Sought out, A city not forsaken* (Isaiah 62:11-12, KJV).

REPENT, REQUEST, AND RESIST

The written proclamation contained in every stake driven into the ground of these cities contains this declaration made by God's lawful representatives of that city:

> "On the basis of scripture, I stand for leaders of this city, and I stand as a representative for other city pastors who desire to do three things, *repent, request and resist.*
>
> We *repent...* we ask the Lord to forgive us for the sins that have taken place in this state and this region, specifically this city. We ask for forgiveness of the sins of political corruption, racial prejudice, moral perversions, witchcraft,

occult and idolatry. We pray the blood of Jesus to cleanse our hands from the shedding of innocent blood. We ask forgiveness for divisions in the church, forgiveness for pride, forgiveness for the sins of the tongue, anything that has hurt the cause of Christ. We repent and humble ourselves to ask for mercy to be poured out on our land, our community and our churches.

We *request...* we ask for God's kingdom to come, and His will to be done in this city. We ask in the Name of Jesus for an outpouring of grace, and mercy and fire, for true spiritual revival to come and cover the community, causing a turning back to God, a cleansing, and a brokenness, and a humility. We ask for the destiny of this city not to be aborted. We ask that You visit this city and our churches, and our homes. Do not pass this city by. We ask for a restoration of the foundations of righteousness to this city.

We also *resist*, on the basis of my submission to God, by faith I resist the devil and his works, all forces, and all powers of evil that have taken hold of the city. We resist the spirit of wickedness that has established strongholds in this city, the dark places, the hidden works of darkness, the mystery places where the enemy has set up encampments. We call on the name of the Lord to destroy all spiritual strongholds, we proclaim this day that this city, especially this region, is now under the power and ownership of the Holy Spirit. All other spirits are hereby given notice, and evicted from this property by the power of the Name of Jesus. Today we stand in the gap and build a hedge of protection around this city."[1]

Before you ever purchase property in the natural, you need to have it surveyed or staked, and you need to determine if you are willing to pay the price to possess the land. When we stake our cities as God's people, we are in effect declaring open war on satan's kingdom. Our acts are bold acts of outright aggression without apology or hesitation. We're telling the devil, "We have declared this before God, and now we are telling you, 'We will take the city!'"[2]

A word of the Lord has come to me about "old wells" that applies directly to cities as well as to older mainline denominations and churches. God is going to redig or uncap the old wells first, before the newer artesian wells break open. Genesis chapter 26 tells us that Isaac had his men redig the wells that his father, Abraham, had originally dug many years before in the Valley of Gerar. Although his father's enemies had filled in the wells after Abraham's death, Isaac still called them by their original names. He found so much water there that he constantly battled with Philistine raiders and finally moved to Beersheba, or "the well of the oath." It was here that Jacob encountered the living God and discovered his true birthright in God's plan.[3]

In this day, God is uncapping some of the ancient wells of revival. These are places where His glory is like a standing pool of water. People have to come to the well to get satisfied, and that is by God's design. Before God brings forth the new wells, He will redig the old wells.[4] In the year before I began working on writing *The God Chasers,* the Lord spoke to my spirit and said, "I am going to re-visit the places of historical revival to give My people another chance. I will call them to dig out the debris from the old wells so that the starting of the new revival will be upon the foundations of the old revival."

In simple terms, before the real revival breaks out in the malls, it will have to break out in our church altars. Then the back pews. Then is when the glory of the Lord can flow underneath the threshold of the door and out into the streets in fulfillment of the prophecy in Ezekiel 47:

> *Afterward he brought me again unto the door of the*
> *house; and, behold, waters issued out from under the*
> *threshold of the house eastward: for the forefront of the*

house stood toward the east, and the waters came down from under from the right side of the house, at the south side of the altar. Then brought he me out of the way of the gate northward, and led me about the way without unto the utter gate by the way that looketh eastward; and, behold, there ran out waters on the right side. And when the man that had the line in his hand went forth eastward, he measured a thousand cubits, and he brought me through the waters; the waters were to the ankles. Again he measured a thousand, and brought me through the waters; the waters were to the knees. Again he measured a thousand, and brought me through; the waters were to the loins. Afterward he measured a thousand; and it was a river that I could not pass over: for the waters were risen, waters to swim in, a river that could not be passed over. And it shall come to pass, that every thing that liveth, which moveth, whithersoever the rivers shall come, shall live: and there shall be a very great multitude of fish, because these waters shall come thither: for they shall be healed; and every thing shall live whither the river cometh. And by the river upon the bank thereof, on this side and on that side, shall grow all trees for meat, whose leaf shall not fade, neither shall the fruit thereof be consumed: it shall bring forth new fruit according to his months, because their waters they issued out of the sanctuary: and the fruit thereof shall be for meat, and the leaf thereof for medicine (Ezekiel 47:1-5,9,12, KJV).

Isn't it ironic that the river of God's Presence flowing from His sanctuary actually grew deeper the further the prophet walked? Finally Ezekiel ended up in water that was over his head and he couldn't touch bottom. He was out of control. I am after an "out-of-control" revival! Its shallowest point should be at the "church" building!

THE NEXT WAVE OF GLORY

I believe that some cities are old wells of God's anointing—places of historical revival. God is calling pastors and congregations in those cities to redig those wells. Unfortunately, digging the debris out of an old well is not a pleasant task. When a pastor friend of mine bought some property in India, he was told that there was an old well on the property. It wasn't a common "vertical" well; it was slanted horizontally into the side of a mountain.

As the ministry workers began to dig out the debris, they found old machinery, discarded furniture, and mounds of old trash among high stands of overgrown weeds and rushes. They found something else too: They encountered hundreds of cobras in that abandoned well, and they had to be removed. My friend told me, "We got that old well all cleaned out and went to bed. When we got up the next morning, we hoped and expected to find a pool of stagnant water waiting for us. But we discovered that the water in the well had begun to bubble up and was flowing so strongly again that it had created a stream overnight!"

The next wave will come as God uncaps the artesian wells of His glory! Many of the wells in the deserts of the Middle East are "standing pool wells." There is enough water seeping up into the natural holding tank of the earth to keep it filled most of the time, even in the desert heat. Almost every living thing in the desert ecosystem makes its way to the oasis or standing pool well for the water of life. God has uncapped abundant standing pools of His Presence that have brought life to millions of thirsty believers and unsaved people over the last few decades. But they must travel to the well. There is forgotten power in pilgrimage.

Now He is about to release the next stage or wave of His anointing, and it will be unlike the old standing pool wells in that these new wells will be artesian wells that will explode with great force. According to Webster's Ninth New Collegiate Dictionary, an "artesian well" is "a well made by boring into the earth until water is reached which from internal pressure flows up like a fountain; a deep-bored well."[5]

This new wave or level of God's glory will come solely from the "deep-bored" people of God's Presence. It will explode into our world with such force that His life-giving Presence will push beyond every barrier and obstacle to flow into the thirsty streets of our cities and nations. This is how His glory will "cover the whole earth" (see Isa. 6:3; Hab. 2:14). Fountains of the deep will break open!

You don't have to go to the waters of an artesian well; the water goes to you! Given the fact that water always seeks the lowest level and the path of least resistance, it is easy to see why Jesus, the "brightness of [the Father's] glory, and the express image of His person" (Heb. 1:3, KJV), said, "...the poor have the gospel preached to them" (Matt. 11:5, KJV). God's glory always seeks to fill the void in the lives of men. In the days to come, God's glory will emanate from the most confounding places and individuals, and it will begin to flow and fill the lowest and most open of people. And He alone will receive the glory.

The Lord spoke to me clearly about His glory during a rare downpour in Southern California. I was born and raised in Louisiana where we are accustomed to seeing days of rain.

There were many times when it would rain continuously for days and nights and no one would think anything about it. But when it rains in Southern California, people take notice. On this particular day, something strange was going on. California was getting a "Louisiana-style" thunderstorm. It was almost a sub-tropical downpour. Back home, people prepare for rain because they are used to it. They build ditches, culverts, and storm sewers, so they are ready for the rain when it comes.

The Los Angeles area, however, is not accustomed to that much rain. I happened to be in a coffee shop when it began. After twenty minutes had passed, I realized it wasn't going to stop so I went out to where I'd parked the car on the street. The water was flowing over the curb and was almost knee-high in the street! I had to wade through it just to get my car out before the water level rose any higher—in just twenty minutes! As I drove away, I said to myself, "They sure don't build storm drains here or something. I don't know where the rain goes at home, but it never gets that deep in the streets that quick."

As I walked through the rain back to my hotel room, I sensed God's Presence and just began to weep. As tears mingled with the rain, I sensed the Lord speak to my heart, "Just as they are unprepared for the rain in the natural, so are they unprepared for My rain in the Spirit. And I will come upon them suddenly."

As I prepared for the meeting that night, I listened to the local news and heard the weatherman in Los Angeles say something that struck a prophetic nerve in me. He said, "This is not the last storm. Actually, they are stacking up out in the Pacific like waves, one against another." Then he added, "They're just going to keep coming," and explained that the source of those waves of rain was El Niño. El Niño in Spanish means "the babe" and is used to refer to the babe of Bethlehem! That weatherman didn't realize that he was prophesying, but he was talking about the "Christ child," the Source of all the waves of glory about to sweep over this planet.

In that moment, something rose up in me and said, "Yes, Lord! Just send wave after wave of Your glory until it has literally flooded everything! May all that is not of You just be washed away downstream." Rain, Jesus, reign!

Very often the "law of precedent" applies to parallel events in the natural and spiritual realms. I am so hungry for the unleashing of His glory that I can't express its intensity or urgency. So I pray,

> *"Lord, just let it rain! Satan is not going to have enough storm sewers to drain off the glory this time. It's going to rise so high that everybody is going to be floated off their feet and out of control in a mighty wave of the glory of God. Let it rain, Lord!"*

Break open the fountains of the deep.

Uncap the ancient wells.

Reclaim your heritage.

Stake the city!

The earth is the Lord's! He's done it before; He can do it again!

Send the rain, Lord.

ENDNOTES

1. For further information, contact City Bible Church, 9200 N.E. Fremont, Portland, Oregon, 97220.

2. I felt so compelled by this that I, along with a band of intercessors, went to Bonnie Brae Street in Los Angeles, California, which was the site of the original outbreak that grew so large it had to be moved to Azusa Street. While interceding there on the property, we drove in a stake! Something seemed to break in my heart (and, I hope, in the heavenlies). It felt like we were tapping into an old well! Debris was being removed and repented of. May the waters of Azusa flow again.

3. See Genesis 28:10-16.

4. My good friend, Lou Engle, wrote a book on this subject of "redigging the wells," and in it he deals with all the details of intercessory prayer. See Lou Engle, *Digging the Wells of Revival* (Shippensburg, PA: Destiny Image, 1998).

5. *Webster's Ninth New Collegiate Dictionary* (Springfield, MA: Merriam-Webster, Inc., 1988), 105.

REVIVAL PRAYER

What is the key to seeing entire cities transformed by the rain of revival? James W. Goll, both a respected prophet and teacher, has committed his ministry to raising up a people who bombard Heaven with a prayer storm. This is the very kind of prayer we need to be practicing in order to see transformational revival spread!

Prayer is absolutely essential if we are going to "ask for the rain" and see God's movement increase on earth. In one sense, God Almighty is Sovereign King. He will accomplish His purposes with or without our aid. At the same time, the Sovereign One has enlisted us into His service. We have been designated co-laborers with Jesus Christ and ambassadors of reconciliation, bridging the gulf between Heaven and earth for an orphaned planet and people (see 2 Cor. 5:18-21). This was not our idea; it was God's. No man on earth initiated this strategy; it was the good pleasure of the Sovereign King to invite us into His unfolding agenda for creation.

So why pray? Scripture makes a very compelling case for it, hence why James Goll delivered such an urgent call to pray through his book, *Prayer Storm*. We are once again reminded of the illustration in Zechariah 10:1, in which we are told to *ask* for the rain.

Even though we are living in a time of outpouring, we need to ask for more.

Even though we are seeing entire communities of Christians trained, discipled and released for supernatural ministry, we need to keep praying.

Even though we hear of missionaries healing the sick, raising the dead, and seeing the masses receive Christ, we need to keep praying.

Even though everyday believers are going through their everyday lives, operating in the gifts of the Spirit, sharing prophetic words, and releasing the power of God in grocery stores, malls, and other seemingly ordinary places, we need to *keep praying*.

Prayer—and persistent prayer at that—has played an integral role in every recorded move of God throughout history. Why? God is looking for the voice on earth that cries out *amen* to everything Heaven has already said *Yes* to. Revival prayer refuses to let go of God's promises until those promises become released in our lives and cities. You will see a powerful example of this in the prayer efforts that helped birth the Hebrides Revival back in 1949.

The following chapter has been taken from James Goll's book, *Prayer Storm*. For more information on James's prayer resources and movement, visit prayerstorm.com.

CHAPTER 7

PRAYER FOR REVIVAL IN THE CHURCH

James Goll

I will heal their backsliding, I will love them freely: for mine anger is turned away from him. I will be as the dew unto Israel: he shall grow as the lily, and cast forth his roots as Lebanon. His branches shall spread, and his beauty shall be as the olive tree, and his smell as Lebanon. They that dwell under his shadow shall return; they shall revive as the corn, and grow as the vine: the scent thereof shall be as the wine of Lebanon.
—HOSEA 14:4-7, KJV

John Wesley was once asked how he managed to gather such large crowds to listen to him preach. His response was immediate: "I set myself on fire, and people come to watch me burn!"[1] Where does that kind of fire come from? That kind of revival fire is ignited by the burning lampstand of fervent intercession.

What does a fire do? It warms and enlightens. It purifies. It empowers. A spiritual fire does the same things as a natural fire—it warms up a cold heart and makes it desire God. It releases the revelation like rays of light so that, suddenly, it's as if "the lights just came on." It burns sin out and brings cleansing to hearts and souls. And it releases new zeal and power into a believer's life. When we're praying for revival, we're praying for revival fire. We're praying for a firestorm.

WHAT IS REVIVAL?

Only something that was once alive can be revived. In other words, revival isn't the same as birth. You can revive a drowned person, but what you're doing is bringing that person back to the life that he or she already had before they drowned. Revival means the return to life or the recovery from death or apparent death.

Revival also means a return to activity after a season of lethargy, apathy, and languor. It's like a shock to the system. Emotions rise again as spirits are revived. Isaiah portrays this aspect of revival:

> *Oh, that You would rend the heavens and come down,*
> *that the mountains might quake at Your Presence—*
> *as fire kindles the brushwood, as fire causes water to*
> *boil—to make Your name known to Your adversaries,*
> *that the nations may tremble at Your Presence! When*
> *You did awesome things which we did not expect, You*
> *came down, the mountains quaked at Your Presence*
> (Isaiah 64:1-3).

Revival also applies to the recovery of a vital truth from oblivion, neglect, or obscurity, or, in other words, to the return to life of something that has been forgotten. This is easy to see in spiritual terms, because in times of spiritual revival, long-neglected truths are restored to life, and people rejoice to learn and obey them once again. In a time of revival, people renew their interest in spiritual concerns, their hearts and souls are restored with fresh life, and they are eager to engender more life wherever they go. Spiritual revival is so powerful that society itself can be transformed.

Colin Dye, whose church, Kensington Temple, in London, England, is one of the largest churches in Europe, is a scholar and a statesman as well as a pastor. Here is what he says about revival:

> Revival is a season of a powerful visitation from God. The term, properly speaking, belongs to the history of the Church subsequent to the New Testament era. However, during the historic revivals we can identify dominant elements that are also present in the New Testament Church. These center on God acting through powerful manifestations of His Presence, strengthening the Church, and awakening the world. Indeed, there are many features of revival that flow out of the New Testament experience of God: conviction of sin, many conversions, powerful spiritual encounters, revelations of God, great assurance of salvation, spiritual fervor, and some kind of lasting legacy for the Church and society at large.[2]

You see here that revival involves a visitation from God in which His Presence is powerfully and tangibly manifested in order to strengthen the Church and awaken the sleeping world to His reality. People in the midst of revival are convicted of sin, converted to faith, impressed with God's truth, and propelled into firsthand experiences of a spiritual nature—and this has lasting results.

In the Bible, we can find prayers for revival. I have already quoted Isaiah's impassioned plea for God to "rend the heavens and come down." The sons of Korah, who were psalmists, and the prophet Habakkuk also prayed for God's life to be rekindled in the lives of His people:

> *You showed favor to Your land, O Lord; You restored*
> *the fortunes of Jacob. You forgave the iniquity of Your*

people and covered all their sins. Selah. You set aside all Your wrath and turned from Your fierce anger. Restore us again, O God our Savior, and put away Your displeasure toward us. Will You be angry with us forever? Will You prolong Your anger through all generations? Will You not revive us again, that Your people may rejoice in You? (Psalm 85:1-6, NIV).

Lord, I have heard of Your fame; I stand in awe of Your deeds, O Lord. Renew them in our day, in our time make them known; in wrath remember mercy (Habakkuk 3:2, NIV).

These Scriptures are like "prayer ammo." We can use them over and over.

PRAYER AND THE HEBRIDES REVIVAL

Before the revival in the Hebrides islands off Scotland, in 1949, two elderly sisters and several young men prayed those words from Isaiah 64:1 over and over for weeks and months: "Lord, rend the heavens and come down!" They also prayed from the words of Isaiah 44:3-4:

For I will pour water upon him that is thirsty, and floods upon the dry ground: I will pour My spirit upon thy seed, and My blessing upon thine offspring: And they shall spring up as among the grass, as willows by the water courses (Isaiah 44:3-4, KJV).

Their fervent pleas were rewarded when God's Spirit fell on the islands to such a degree that spontaneous conversions occurred everywhere and the crime rate plummeted. It became one of the most phenomenal outpourings of the Holy Spirit since the Day of Pentecost.

The sisters, Christine and Peggy Smith, 82 and 84 years old, were too frail to leave their cottage, located in the village of Barvas on the island of Lewis, to attend worship services. Peggy was blind, and Christine was crippled with arthritis. So they prayed from home. They prayed twice a week. They would get on their knees at ten o'clock in the evening, and they never stopped praying until three or four o'clock in the morning.

After God gave them a vision of revival in their parish church, a group of young men who were office-holders in the parish began to pray as well, and they prayed together twice a week in a cold barn, on Tuesday and Friday nights. Sometimes the men were forced to crawl inside of the haystacks in order to keep warm. Under the inspiration of the Holy Spirit, these nine ordinary Scots prayed without a letup for a month and a half, pleading with God to send revival to their community and beyond.

One night, a deacon stood up and read from Psalm 24:

> *Who shall ascend into the hill of the Lord? Or who shall stand in His holy place? He that hath clean hands, and a pure heart; who hath not lifted up his soul unto vanity, nor sworn deceitfully. He shall receive the blessing [notice that it's "the" blessing, not "a" blessing] from the Lord, and righteousness from the God of his salvation. This is the generation of them that seek Him, that seek Thy face, O Jacob* (Psalm 24:3-6 KJV).

Before he sat down, he challenged his fellow intercessors—and himself—by asking God, "God, are my hands clean? Is my heart pure?" He could not go any further, because he fell on the floor of the barn under the power of the Spirit. All of those present were convicted of how essential holiness was to those who would expect a visitation from God.

Soon after, the elderly sisters urged their pastor to bring in an evangelist, because in a vision, one of them had seen a man who was not from their village speaking in the pulpit. After a series of inquiries, he brought a young man named Duncan Campbell to speak.

Here is a small portion of Campbell's own account of what happened on the very first night, told almost 20 years later. Here is what happened just after he had finished preaching to a congregation of about three hundred people.

> Just as I am walking down the aisle, along with this young deacon who read the Psalm in the barn, he suddenly stood in the aisle and looking up to the heavens he said: "God, You can't fail us. God, You can't fail us. You promised to pour water on the thirsty and floods upon the dry ground—God, You can't fail us!"
>
> Soon he is on his knees in the aisle, and he is still praying, and then he falls into a trance again. Just then the door opened—it is now eleven o'clock. The door of the church opens, and the local blacksmith comes back into the church and says, "Mr. Campbell, something wonderful has happened. Oh, we were praying that God would pour water on the thirsty and floods upon the dry ground and listen, He's done it! He's done it!"
>
> When I went to the door of the church I saw a congregation of approximately 600 people. Six hundred people—where had they come from? What had happened? I believe that that very night God swept in Pentecostal power—the power of the Holy Ghost. And what happened in the early days of the apostles was happening now in the parish of Barvas.
>
> Over 100 young people were at the dance in the parish hall and they weren't thinking of God or eternity. God was not in all of their thoughts. They were there to have a good night when suddenly the power of God fell upon the dance. The music ceased, and in a matter of minutes, the hall was empty. They fled from the hall as a man fleeing from a plague. And they made for the church. They are now standing outside. Oh, yes—they saw lights in the

church. That was a house of God and they were going to it and they went. Men and women who had gone to bed rose, dressed, and made for the church. Nothing in the way of publicity—no mention of a special effort except an intonation from the pulpit on Sabbath that a certain man was going to be conducting a series of meetings in the parish covering 10 days. But God took the situation in hand—oh, He became His own publicity agent. A hunger and a thirst gripped the people. 600 of them now are at the church standing outside.[3]

Duncan Campbell far exceeded the ten-day time period he had agreed to stay. The first wave of the revival lasted five weeks. Prayer meetings were held day and night throughout the parishes. Then there was a brief lull, followed by weeks more. The revival was not accompanied by healings or by speaking in tongues, but everyone experienced remarkable, repeated, power-encounters with God. Bold prayers were prayed—and answered. Incorrigible sinners were saved, many of whom went on to lead many others to Christ. An astonishing number of those who were saved were young people, very few of whom ever stopped following Jesus for the rest of their lives, and many of whom are still alive today, of course, because all of this happened only in the middle of the 20th century.[4]

The reason I tell you this story is because it helps answer the question, "What is revival?" Although the specifics may differ from place to place and from time to time, some of them will always be present in a true revival, not the least of which is always fervent, concentrated, persistent intercessory prayer.

THE ROLE OF PRAYER IN SPIRITUAL AWAKENING

Without prayer, revival will not come. But what does this kind of prayer look like? In 1976, an Oxford-educated church historian named

J. Edwin Orr gave a talk entitled "The Role of Prayer in Spiritual Awakening" at the National Prayer Congress in Dallas. A videotape of his presentation was made, and it is still available today. Here are some excerpts from it:

> Dr. A.T. Pierson once said, "There has never been a spiritual awakening in any country or locality that did not begin in united prayer." Let me recount what God has done through concerted, united, sustained prayer.
>
> Not many people realize that in the wake of the American Revolution there was a moral slump.... [Crime, drunkenness, profanity rose to alarming levels. Churches stopped growing and began to shrink.] Christians were so few on [the campuses of Ivy League colleges] in the 1790s that they met in secret, like a communist cell, and kept their minutes in code so that no one would know.... The Chief of Justice of the United States, John Marshall, wrote to the Bishop of Virginia, James Madison, that the Church "was too far gone ever to be redeemed." Voltaire averred, and Tom Paine echoed, "Christianity will be forgotten in thirty years."
>
> ...How did the situation change? It came through a concert of prayer.... In New England, there was a man of prayer named Isaac Backus, a Baptist pastor who in 1794, when conditions were at their worst, addressed an urgent plea for prayer for revival to pastors of every Christian denomination in the United States.
>
> Churches knew that their backs were to the wall, so the Presbyterians of New York, New Jersey, and Pennsylvania adopted it for all their churches. Bishop Francis Asbury adopted it for all the Methodists. The Congregational and Baptist Associations, the Reformed and the Moravians all adopted the plan, until America...was interlaced with a

network of prayer meetings, which set aside the first Monday of each month to pray.

It was not too long before the revival came. It broke out first of all in Connecticut, then spread to Massachusetts and all the seaboard states, in every case entirely without extravagance or outcry. [In the summer of 1800, when it reached Kentucky, which was a lawless territory at the time, it burst into wildfire. Great camp meetings were held, and pastors of every denominational affiliation assisted when as many as 11,000 people came to one communion service.]

Out of that second great awakening...came the whole modern missionary movement and its societies. Out of it came the abolition of slavery, popular education, Bible societies, Sunday schools and many social benefits....

[However, by the mid-1800s, conditions had deteriorated again.] In September 1857, a man of prayer, Jeremiah Lanphier, started a prayer meeting in the upper room of the Dutch Reformed Church consistory building in Manhattan. In response to his advertisement, only six people out of the population of a million showed up. But, the following week, there were fourteen, and then twenty-three, when it was decided to meet every day for prayer. By late winter, they were filling the Dutch Reformed Church, then the Methodist Church on John Street, then Trinity Episcopal Church on Broadway at Wall Street. In February and March of 1858, every church and public hall in downtown New York was filled. Horace Greeley, the famous editor, sent a reporter with horse and buggy racing around the prayer meetings to see how many men were praying: in one hour, he could get to only twelve meetings, but he counted 6100 men attending. Then a landslide of prayer began, which overflowed to the churches in the evenings. People began to be converted, ten thousand a week in New York City alone. The movement spread throughout New England, the church bells bringing people to prayer at eight in the morning, twelve noon, six in the evening. The revival raced up the Hudson and down the Mohawk, where the Baptists, for example, had so many people to baptize that they went down to the river, cut a big hole in the ice, and baptized them in the cold water: when Baptists do that they really are on fire.... [Out of this revival came a young shoe salesman whose name became a household word, D.L. Moody.] ...More than a million people were converted to God in one year out of a population of thirty million.

Then that same revival jumped the Atlantic and appeared in Ulster, Scotland, Wales, then England, parts of Europe, South Africa and South India, anywhere there was an evangelical cause. It sent mission pioneers to many countries. Effects were felt for forty years. Having begun in a movement of prayer, it was sustained by a movement of prayer.

That movement lasted for a generation, but at the turn of the twentieth century, there was need of awakening again. A general movement of prayer began, with special prayer meetings at Moody Bible Institute; at Keswick Convention in England; and places as far apart as Melbourne, Australia; Wonsan in Korea; and Nilgiri Hills of India. So all around the world believers were praying that there might be another great awakening in the twentieth century....

[Among the most notable results of this prayer is the well-known Welsh Revival of 1904]. ...The movement went like a tidal wave over Wales. In five months there were a hundred thousand people converted throughout the country.... It was the social impact that was astounding. For example, judges were presented with white gloves, not a case to try: no robberies, no burglaries, no rapes, no murders and no embezzlements, nothing.... As the revival swept Wales, drunkenness was cut in half. There was a wave of bankruptcies, but they were nearly all for taverns. There was even a slowdown in the mines. You say, "How could a religious revival cause a strike?" It did not cause a strike, just a slowdown, for so many Welsh coal miners were converted and stopped using bad language that the horses that dragged the trucks in the mines could not understand what was being said to them, hence transportation slowed down for a while until they learned the language of Canaan. (When I first heard that story, I thought that it was a tall tale, but I can document it.) That revival also affected sexual moral standards, I had discovered through the figures given by British government experts that, in Radnorshire and Merionethshire, the actual illegitimate birth rate had dropped 44% within a year of the beginning of the revival. That revival swept Britain. It so moved all of Norway that the Norwegian Parliament passed special legislation to permit laymen to conduct Communion because the clergy could not keep up with the number of the converts desiring to partake. It swept Sweden, Finland and Denmark, Germany, Canada from coast to coast, all of the United States, Australia, New Zealand, South Africa, East Africa, Central Africa, West Africa, touching also Brazil, Mexico, and Chile....

As always, it began through a movement of prayer, with prayer meetings all over the United States as well as the other countries; and soon there came the great time of the harvest. So what is the lesson we can learn? It is a very simple one, as direct as the promises of God in Scripture: "If My people, who are called by My name, shall humble themselves and pray, and seek My face, and turn from their wicked ways, then I will hear from heaven and will forgive their sin and will heal their land" (2 Chron. 7:14, RSV).

What is involved in this? As God requires us to pray, we must not forget what was said by Jonathan Edwards: "...to promote explicit agreement and visible union of God's people in extraordinary prayer." What do we mean by extraordinary prayer? We share in ordinary prayer in regular worship services, before eating and the like. But when people are found getting up at six in the morning to pray, or having a half night of prayer until midnight, or giving up their lunchtime to pray at a noonday prayer meeting, that is extraordinary prayer. But it must be united and concerted.[5]

Dr. Orr touched on just a few highlights from the 19th and 20th centuries. Again and again, we see the powerful effect of prayer in bringing about true revival. It takes a lot of prayer to bring true revival. It takes an army of intercessors praying over time. Those who pray for revival do not need to be in the same room at the same time, although sometimes they are. They don't even need to speak the same language, because they might come from different countries. But they do need to be united in purpose: "Lord, send Your Spirit. Revive us again! Rend the heavens and come down!"

REVIVAL PRELIMINARIES

Prayer is an absolute prerequisite for revival. It stems from a hunger and an intense desire for *change*. Something simply must change in the situation, because the situation is intolerable. Or—tell me if you have not experienced this yourself—it's more as if something must change in the situation, because the situation is just plain boring! You know what I mean. You have gone along for some time, and nothing has seemed very exciting. Church just isn't quite meeting your needs. You can't figure out what your purpose is, and you're not sure the people around you know what theirs is either. You can't quite put your finger on what's wrong, but you get frustrated with it. In times like these, your heart and mouth can release grumbling and accusation—or prayer. If you want to get out of the doldrums and into revival, choose prayer. Prayer definitely changes things.

Another prerequisite for revival is networking. People begin to pull together in *unity*. They begin to pool their efforts and their prayers. They begin to cry out with one voice: "Lord, we need You! We are hungry for You. We are utterly dependent upon You." The relational work of networking results in progress toward unified prayer with an identifiable goal. Praying as a team gives feet to your restlessness and hope in the midst of your spiritual hunger.

In the Nashville area where I live, different congregations and ministries host a Call2Worship periodically on Sunday nights. It's just a small piece of the big picture, but it's an important one. It builds citywide unity, promotes hunger for the Lord, and releases the power of corporate worship and prayer. Those prayers hit their targets! They don't just bounce off the ceiling. What makes the difference is that we pray together; we have united across denominational and cultural lines to seek God's face for the sake of our city and region.

WHAT REVIVAL LOOKS LIKE

Prayer is a key ingredient prior to revival, and prayer continues as a key ingredient for sustaining the results of revival. What are we looking for when we pray for revival? And what does it look like to sustain revival when the Holy Spirit brings it?

There are five primary characteristics of true, classic revival: (1) an experiential conviction of sin, which results in (2) a passionate denunciation of sin, because of (3) a revelation of God's holiness, (4) a deep awareness of God's love and mercy, and (5) a sometimes painfully heightened consciousness of eternity. These characteristics can be illustrated abundantly from the Scriptures and from the history of the ebb and flow of the Christian faith.

For example, David Brainerd, who went out into the forests and preached to the natives in early America, prayed for days at a time, outdoors. He longed to portray the Lord Jesus Christ as a kind and compassionate master, and he would intercede and plead with his listeners to accept the mercy of God—and they did. Even though Brainerd's life was cut short, most likely because of the hardships he endured, the results of his prayer and preaching brought the Kingdom to a people group who had lived in spiritual darkness for generations.

A classic example from the same time period is Jonathan Edwards, whose prayers and sermons helped to usher in the First Great Awakening in colonial America. His preaching was not "seeker friendly," but seekers—often with much emotion—did find salvation at the feet of the living God. Edwards's most famous sermon is titled, "Sinners in the Hands of an Angry God," and others bear such appealing titles as "Wrath Upon the Wicked for the Uttermost," "Eternity of Hell's Torments," and "Justice of God in the Damnation of Sinners." Edwards's passion was not so much that sin would be exposed and punished as it was that God's overwhelming mercy would be given an opportunity to reach people's hearts. The heart-revival that he spearheaded swept across the colonies and effected broad societal changes, influencing the future spiritual climate of an entire continent.

PRAYER BEFORE REVIVAL, DURING REVIVAL, AND AFTER REVIVAL

Prayer, and more prayer, is the appropriate response to desperate times. Extreme prayer at all hours of the day and night is the only appropriate application of effort before, during, and after a time of revival from God. God wants to revive His people, wherever they may live. In other words, revival is *His* work, and the way we participate is to engage *Him* in all prayerfulness.

Charles Finney, who was known for his phenomenal evangelistic successes during the Second Great Awakening in the United States, had equally phenomenal prayer support behind the scenes. He is quoted as having said, "Revival is no more a miracle than a crop of wheat. Revival comes from heaven when heroic souls enter the conflict determined to win or die—or if need be, to win and die."[6]

Matthew Henry, an English theologian and clergyman who predates Finney, Edwards, and Brainerd and who composed the massive commentaries to the Old and New Testaments that bear his name, wrote, "When God intends to do great mercy for his people, the first thing he does is to set them a-praying."[7]

Not just any kind of prayer will do. This kind of praying makes you sweat. It is hard work. It's often compared to the travail of childbirth. Leonard Ravenhill, a 20th-century British revivalist, once said, "At God's counter there are no sale days, for the price for revival is ever the same—travail."[8]

E.M. Bounds, a Civil-War-era preacher and author who wrote prolifically about the importance of prayer, especially as it applies to all forms and stages of revival, wrote,

> The wrestling quality of importunate prayer does not spring from physical vehemence or fleshly energy. It is not an impulse of energy, nor mere earnestness of soul. It is an inwrought force, a faculty implanted and aroused by the Holy Spirit. Virtually, it is the intercession of the Holy Spirit in us.[9]

Bounds had laid hold of the same truth that Jesus expressed to His disciples: "...The kingdom of heaven suffers violence and the violent take it by force" (Matt. 11:12, NKJV).

Prayer for revival, which is one of the four primary emphases of Prayer Storm, is prayer for the Kingdom of God to come *here* and *now*. The only effective prayer is that which is inspired by the Holy Spirit, and that prayer, by definition, is going to be "violent," passionate, and untiringly persistent.

This kind of prayer will incur opposition. Persecution, opposition, and challenge are guaranteed. No advance of the Kingdom goes unchallenged; what you challenge will challenge you back. If you target individuals in prayer, persecution will come to you from individuals. If you target the Church in prayer, opposition will come from the Church. If you target the society around you, some segment of that society will fight back.

Therefore, you need even more fervency and even more of the Spirit of revival. Like those who have gone before you, you need to press forward, undaunted, linked arm in arm and spirit to spirit with your fellow intercessors, walking together through the conflict with other prayer warriors until victory is achieved. And then, after revival has come, you must support each other in the great work of stewarding the longed-for move of God.

> *In the name of Jesus, we labor with His Holy Spirit for a God-sent revival in our day. We will not quit praying until we have seen with our own eyes the glory of the Lord covering the earth as the waters cover the seas. O God, release a global revival to the Church in our day! Awaken the sleeping beauty called the body of Christ to her destiny. Start in our nation! Start in my city! Start in my congregation! Start in my family! Start in my very own heart! Release revival fire for the sake of Your holy name! Amen and Amen.*

ENDNOTES

1. John Wesley.
2. Colin Dye, teaching notes, quoted in James W. Goll, *Revival Breakthrough Study Guide* (Franklin, TN: Encounters Network, 2000), 43.

3.   Duncan Campbell, "Revival in the Hebrides (1949)" (1969), transcript available at *Shilohouse Ministries*, http://www. shilohouse .org/Hebrides_Revival.htm (accessed 19 April 2008).

4.   The story of the Hebrides Revival has been published in many places. Many of these details came from the Campbell transcript.

5.   J. Edwin Orr, "Prayer and Revival," at http://www.jedwinorr.com/ prayer_revival.htm.

6.   Charles Finney, for this description of revival, see "What a Revival of Religion Is," http://www.gospeltruth.net/ 1868Lect_on_Rev_of _Rel/68revlec01.htm.

7.   From commentary on Isaiah 62:6-9; Matthew Henry, *Commentary on the Whole Bible, Vol. IV* (Isaiah to Malachi), 2nd ed., (Peabody, MA: Hendrickson Publishers, 1991).

8.   Leonard Ravenhill, *Why Revival Tarries* (Bloomington, MN: Bethany House, 1979), 138.

9.   E.M. Bounds, *The Necessity of Prayer* (Grand Rapids, MI: Baker Publishing Group, 1979), 63.

Truly, God has raised Banning Liebscher up for "such a time" to mobilize a new generation of revivalists. Continuing on with the topic of Revival Prayer, it is vital for those asking for the rain of revival to build a history with God in the "secret place" of His Presence.

How does one become gripped with a burden for revival? Intimate union with God.

How does one become like the great prayer warriors of old, persisting and pressing in for outpouring, even when morality is declining, the church is backsliding, and all hope seems lost?

Prayer warriors are cultivated, not born. They are forged in the fires of spiritual discontentment. Even though they refuse to turn a blind eye to the present conditions, they persist in prayer in spite of what they see because they have been captured by the heart of God. Imprisoned by His purposes. They know beyond the shadow of any doubt that Heaven's will is to break into the earth with such force, power, outpouring, and awakening, that no church will be able to contain the movement. Walls will not be able to restrict or restrain the masses who rise up to carry God into their unique spheres of influence.

Before Jesus Culture was a global revival movement or an internationally recognized worship band, it was a young adult/youth community in Redding, CA that decided to be committed to revival—no matter what the cost. No matter how long, how hard, or how relentless the efforts needed to be, Banning and his team had said their *yes* to revival. They didn't say *yes* because God assured them of success, fame or notoriety; they said *yes* because they were not content to let the land remain "dry and weary" when there was a River to be released.

The following chapter is from Banning Liebscher's book, *Jesus Culture.*

CHAPTER 8

THE SECRET PLACE

Banning Liebscher

A fire for prayer ignited in my heart when Lou Engle came to Bethel Church or the first time. My journey had begun a few years earlier, but that night I received an impartation from Lou that launched my prayer life to another level. In that meeting, I decided to be a man of prayer. I wanted, as David declared in one of his psalms, to "give myself to prayer" (Ps. 109:4). I read about Frank Bartleman, the intercessor for the Azusa Street Revival, and how a "spirit of intercession had so possessed (him) that (he) prayed almost day and night."[1] He wrote in his book, *Another Wave of Revival*, that his "life was by this time literally swallowed up in prayer. I was praying day and night.... Prayer literally consumed me."[2]

CONSUMED BY PRAYER

I desperately wanted to be "consumed" with prayer, but I knew I needed to learn how. I began to devour books on prayer and biographies of those who prayed—E.M. Bounds, Andrew Murray, Arthur

Wallis, St. Teresa of Avila, Brother Lawrence, Frank Bartleman, Dr. Paul Yonggi Cho, and Leonard Ravenhill. I couldn't read enough about prayer. I was gripped by the stories of men and women who gave themselves to a life of prayer, and I wanted to follow in their footsteps.

Though I learned much from the testimonies of these saints, eventually I came to realize something. The best way to learn to pray is to pray. It's much like learning to be a parent. You can read countless books on the subject of parenting and glean wisdom from multiple experts, but the real learning begins the moment your beautiful child takes his or her first breath. That's when you enter your opening class in Parenting 101. Although I have read books on prayer, listened to sermons on prayer, and talked to people who pray, I learned to pray by actually setting time aside to pray and allowing the Lord Himself to teach me.

Jesus's disciples discovered this truth about prayer as well, as Andrew Murray explains in his book *With Christ in the School of Prayer*:

> The disciples had learned to understand something of the connection between Christ's wondrous life in public and His secret life of prayer. They had been with Him and had seen Him pray. They had learned to believe in Him as a Master in the art of prayer. None could pray like Him. And so they went to Him with the request, "Lord, teach us to pray."[3]

As I drew near to God during my own prayers in the months following Lou's visit to Bethel, I found myself making the same request of the Lord: "Lord, teach [me] to pray" (Luke 11:1). In response, He began to meet with me in prayer in a way I had not previously experienced. I started waking up early in the morning and slipping away to the Alabaster House—the prayer chapel at Bethel. I found that I felt *alive* in prayer. I also began to experience the reality Jesus spoke of when He said, "But you, when you pray, go into your room, and when you have shut your door, pray to your Father who is in the secret place" (Matt. 6:6). God was waiting for me in the secret place of prayer! I entered a realm of God I never before imagined was available. At the time I didn't know it, but I was establishing what Mahesh Chavda describes as my "secret history with the Lord." God was meeting me in the secret place. E.M. Bounds describes it this way: "The man—God's man—is made in the closet. His life and his most profound convictions are born in his secret communion with God."[4]

BUILDING HISTORY WITH GOD IN THE SECRET PLACE

A history was developing between God and me that was not for anyone else. It was outside of the spotlight; no one really even knew it existed. What God and I were sharing in the secret place was not for any external ministry purpose. I just wanted more of Him and discovered that He also wanted simply to spend time with me. I spent hours in the secret place encountering His Presence, worshiping Him, and hearing Him speak to me.

God is waiting to encounter you in your secret place. He longs for a secret history with you. In my wife SeaJay's college years, she had a closet where the Lord would meet her. It was just a walk-in closet, with clothes strewn all over the floor and shirts on hangers, but God was in that closet. SeaJay says that when she pulled away and walked into her closet, she became aware that God was waiting to meet her there. She would sit on her beanbag and wait to see what God wanted to do. Sometimes the Lord invited her simply to rest in the safety of His Presence, and she would curl up and go to sleep. Other times He would take her into intercession through tears. And at times God took her away to a place He had made just for her. It was in the secret place that SeaJay learned to hear and trust her Father and know His ways. She was establishing a private history with God. SeaJay was experiencing what Andrew Murray calls us to: "To be alone in secret with the Father should be your highest joy,"[5] because, "to the man who withdraws himself from all that is of the world and man and waits for God alone, the Father will reveal Himself."[6]

I remember having a similar experience when I went to Bethel's Alabaster House early in the morning to pray. Many times I walked in to find that no one was around. As I opened the doors, tears would begin to stream down my face because I was walking into a room where I knew God was waiting for me. Your secret place may not be an exact location, but you enter it when you pull away from the world and find a place where you and God can establish a secret history together. It may involve spending hours in one location or only moments when you drop what you are doing and simply turn your heart to the One you've been longing for.

The new breed of revivalist emerging in the earth must be a generation that has established a secret life with Christ. The Lord is releasing an anointing to see entire cities and nations turn to Him, but that anointing can be secured only in the secret place. In Second Kings 9, before Jehu was sent to end the reign of Jezebel he had to first get into the inner room to have oil poured on him. This represents the anointing of the Holy Spirit. Arthur Wallis points out that "there can be no substitute whatever for the anointing of the Holy Spirit; it is the one indispensable factor for the effective proclamation of God's message."[7]

There are some things you cannot get in public; you must press in for them in private. You can't go to conferences or have anointed men and women of God lay their hands on you to get this anointing. It is an anointing that results from encountering the Anointed One in the secret place, the inner room of prayer. It's crucial that you go to conferences and have anointed people lay their hands on you, but you won't fully step into everything God has for you until you learn how to separate yourself to the Lord in prayer. Not one revivalist I have ever read about or met acquired his or her anointing through public gatherings. It was received in the secret place of prayer. All of them have (or had) a secret life with God that, for the most part, they don't even talk about.

Lou Engle unintentionally gives us a peek into his secret life of prayer with God through a humorous story he tells. Lou is a general of prayer. He has an anointing to fill stadiums with praying believers and shift nations through intercession. For twenty years he gave his life to crying out for revival in the secret place with God. To this day, his heart burns to be in the secret place with God. His custom is to slip out of bed early in the morning and find a place to be alone with the Lord in prayer. Lou has seven incredible children, so you can imagine how challenging it is to find a secret place in his home! Often he jumps in his van and drives somewhere to pray.

One particular morning, he chose the parking lot of a local convenience store as his prayer closet. If you've seen Lou at all, you know he rocks back and forth while he prays. He says he's "priming the pump" as he rocks. On this occasion, he was having an amazing time in prayer and worship when he was startled by a knock on his window. Looking up, Lou saw a firefighter standing by the window and two large fire trucks parked behind his van. He turned his worship music down, rolled down his window, and curiously asked what was going on. The confused firefighter told him they had received an emergency call at their station about a man in a parked van who was having a seizure. Lou had to explain to the firefighter that he was not having a seizure; he was praying. It's one of my all-time favorite stories. Beyond being funny, it unveils the reality that Lou's life is fueled by prayer in the secret place with God.

Revivalists of the past established their lives in prayer and are shining examples of what God can do with one who prays. John Wesley spent two hours a day in prayer. E.M. Bounds writes of him, "One who knew him well wrote, 'He thought prayer to be more his business than anything else, and I have seen him come out of the closet with a serenity of face next to shining.'"[8]

Martin Luther, the father of the Reformation, said, "If I fail to spend two hours in prayer each morning, the devil gets the victory through the day. I have so much business I cannot get on without spending three hours daily in prayer."[9]

Evan Roberts, the young leader of the Welsh Revival, was a man of prayer. He would slip out of the revival meetings late at night "to pray all night in the quiet of his room."[10] S.B. Shaw recounts a three-month experience Roberts had:

> I was awakened every night a little after one o'clock. This was most strange, for through the years I slept like a rock, and no disturbance in my room would awaken me. From that hour I was taken into divine fellowship for about four hours. What it was I cannot tell you, except that it was divine. About five o'clock I was again allowed to sleep on till about nine. At this time I was again taken up into the same experience as in the earlier hours of the morning until about twelve o'clock.[11]

Before this encounter, Roberts was a man of prayer, but after this extended season of visitation with the Lord, Roberts's prayer life was set ablaze at another level.

David Matthews, a participant in the revival, writes of Roberts, "Day and night, without ceasing, he prayed, wept, and sighed for a great spiritual awakening for his beloved Wales."[12]

Kathryn Kuhlman, more than anyone I've read about, had captured the secret of a life given to prayer—not in the normal sense, for even some of her closest friends don't remember her having a regularly established time of prayer, but a heart that was always turned to the Lord in prayer. She said of her prayer life, "I've learned to commune with the Lord any time, any place. I take my prayer closet with me on the plane, in the car, or walking down the street. I pray always. My life is prayer."[13] Jamie Buckingham, her friend and biographer, writes of a time he saw her in a hallway behind stage before she ministered to the thousands who had come to receive a touch from God, "She was pacing, back and forth, head up, head down, arms flung into the air, hands clasped behind her back. Her face was covered in tears, and as she approached I could hear her. 'Gentle Jesus, take not your Holy Spirit from me.'"[14]

As I mentioned earlier, the prayer life of Jesus was the model and inspiration for His disciples, as it was for every one of these notable revivalists. Jesus was a Man of prayer and had a secret life with the Father. Luke 5:16 states, "But Jesus Himself would often slip away to the wilderness and pray" (NASB). Mark 1:35 states, "Now in the morning, having risen a long while before daylight, He went out and departed to a solitary place; and there He prayed" (NKJV).

My prayer is that there would be a generation of seekers who not only pursue Him corporately but also inquire of Him in the secret place of prayer. I'm encouraged when I see thousands of young people seeking the Lord together, but what I want to know is if that is happening in their bedrooms when no one else is around. Are they bringing to the corporate gatherings the momentum they have gained in the secret place? Have they captured the revelation that Charles Spurgeon talks about when he describes other work as "mere emptiness compared with our closets"?[15]

It's All about Love

I said earlier that the anointing that God is releasing for revival in this season will be accessed and carried successfully only by those who have established a secret history with the Lord. The primary reason for this is that revival is all about *love*. Signs and wonders, preaching, and any other aspect of supernatural ministry have one purpose only—to demonstrate the love of God to people and invite them into the love relationship He desires to have with them. Those who carry this power and demonstrate it to the world must be those who have that kind of kinship with the Lord. And this exchange is established in private. There are conversations my wife and I have that no one else will ever know about. Jamie Buckingham tells of how his backstage encounter with Kathryn Kuhlman praying ended: "I turned and fled, for I felt I had blundered into the most intimate of all conversations between lovers, and just my Presence was an abomination."[16] This is the goal of our lives and the relationship our hearts yearn for with the Lord.

If you've established a secret harmony with the Lord, then, when revival is happening all around you, your foundation will be in place to steward it. Bill Johnson says, "Many times the busyness that revival brings becomes the enemy of revival."[17] It is easy to fall into a vortex of activity while working for revival—forgetting that revival is all about love. When this happens, our industriousness is disconnected from the thing that both motivates and gives it purpose. Without the supply of love behind our work, we will inevitably grow weary and probably give up. With love established in our lives, however, we will find our energy and passion renewed continually. One of my primary concerns in raising up a generation of revivalists is making sure they know how to pursue God privately as well as corporately.

A secret life with God always brings us back to our original purpose and passion. It recalibrates our heart. Whenever we find ourselves drifting away from the ultimate reason we are alive—to love God and be loved by God—the secret place realigns our priorities with love. It is what "keeps the main thing the main thing" in our lives. Your foundation of love must be deeper and wider than anything else in your life. Shasta Dam, one of Redding's claims to fame, is the second largest concrete gravity dam in America. Its hydraulic height is 522 feet. It holds back the massive amount of water in Lake Shasta, one of the largest man-made lakes in North America. But what is so impressive is not its height but its depth. It reaches 85 feet into the ground and is 543 feet thick at the base. Shasta Dam's base is actually wider than it is tall.[18] Similarly, if you are to step fully into your destiny, the depth of your understanding of the love of God must be incomparably larger than anything else in your life.

CONSTANT PRAYER

A few years ago I was flying back from a visit to the International House of Prayer in Kansas City, Missouri when the Lord spoke to me about establishing prayer in our youth ministry. I had gone to IHOP at the invitation of Dwayne Roberts, the leader of One Thing Ministries at the time, who had asked a handful of young leaders to meet and pray together for a few days. It was my first visit to IHOP. By that time, five years of 24/7 worship and prayer had been offered to the Lord from IHOP, and I was greatly impacted to see a ministry that had found keys for sustaining such a high level of intensity and devotion in prayer for so long.

I'm not sure why, but the Lord regularly speaks to me on planes. I think it might be because I'm closer to Heaven in a plane, but that's just a theory. Anyway, the Lord spoke to me about calling our entire youth ministry to give ourselves to prayer during the summer months. We called it "Summer of Prayer"; we scheduled prayer meetings throughout the week, and we began to pray. The first meeting we had was on a Tuesday morning. Only a few people showed up, but we prayed, God came, and it was incredible!

About an hour into our prayer time, we began to pray for the school campuses in our city. I felt myself enter into a realm of authority over these campuses that was unfamiliar to me. It is sometimes difficult to explain feelings or experiences in prayer because it's in the spirit realm. But as I was praying, I could sense a shift in the atmosphere of our prayers, and they seemed to transition from the strength of a small hammer to a power-loaded demolition jackhammer! We knew the spiritual atmosphere was shifting over the campuses as we prayed and that principalities and powers were being displaced. I had touched that realm before, but I understood I didn't live there. Theologically I occupied that spiritual place, but not always in practice. I believed I had been given authority over cities, but I had not pressed into or remained in that realm of authority through prayer. It became clear to me that there are realms of authority only accessed through consistent prayer. I had been praying for years, but I realized there was another level of prayer I had to press into if I was going to access the realm of dominion necessary to see entire cities saved.

What I experienced at that first prayer meeting continued through the summer as we gave ourselves to prayer. During this season we were reminded of a dream that Lance Jacobs, Bethel's outreach pastor at the time, had had a few years earlier. In the dream, Lance was releasing people to minister in the city, but was having no results. Nobody got saved, healed, or delivered. Then Linda McIntosh, one of our youth pastors and the resident lead intercessor, appeared next to Lance and said, "We must pray!" When she declared that, two fighter jets flew overhead. Lance then sent his team out into the city again, and this time the results were drastically different. People were getting saved, miracles were breaking out, and lives were being set free. We knew the Lord was calling us to a higher realm of authority that we had not tapped into yet—a realm that could only be accessed through prayer.

As I said, we found out right away that the cry of our hearts had to be *consistent* if we were to live in those new realms of authority. Jesus emphasized this repeatedly in His teachings on prayer. After instructing His disciples in the Lord's Prayer, He told them a story about someone asking a neighbor for bread at night. He said:

> *I say to you, though he will not rise and give to him because he is his friend, yet because of his **persistence** he will rise and give him as many as he needs. So I say to you, ask, and it will be given to you; seek, and you will find; knock, and it will be opened to you. For everyone who asks receives, and he who seeks finds, and to him who knocks it will be opened* (Luke 11:8-10, NKJV).

The verbs in verse 9 are all in present tense and could be translated, "Ask and continue to ask. Seek and continue to seek. Knock and keep on knocking." We are to persist in asking, seeking, and knocking.

Jesus likewise taught through His parable about the persistent widow "that men always ought to pray and not lose heart" (Luke 18:1). These stories and teachings of Christ took on greater relevance and significance for us as we experienced the power of consistent prayer.

The book of Acts also provides us with a dramatic lesson on the importance of consistent prayer. Acts 12:2 records the death of James, the first apostle to be martyred, at the hands of King Herod. When he saw that James's death made the Jews happy, Herod detained Peter in prison with the intention of killing him as well. The church, mourning the loss of James, was not going to lose another one of their friends and leaders. Their response to the imprisonment of Peter was to pray: "But constant prayer was offered to God for him by the church" (Acts 12:5). Notice that it was not just prayer but *constant prayer*. That night, Peter was miraculously set free by an angel and reunited with the friends who had been praying for him. Continuous prayer was the key for the church of Acts believers to gain access to the realm of authority that was needed to see Peter set free.

It is important to remember that steadfast prayer isn't a matter of trying to convince God to answer us. If anyone knows God's attitude toward us in prayer it is Christ, who declares, "And whatever things you ask in prayer, believing, you will receive" (Matt. 21:22, NKJV). What a staggering statement! Sit back and let that verse hit you. Whatever things we ask will be ours if we believe. The Lord gave us a blank check, signed by Him, and promises that all the resources of Heaven are available to us if we pray. Andrew Murray writes, "The powers of the eternal world have been placed at prayer's disposal."[19] Yet Jesus clearly taught us that prayer must be sustained. If incessant prayer isn't required to get something to happen on God's end, we must conclude that it is required because of what it does on our end. Of course, much of what is going on when we pray is unseen and outside of our awareness. But the truth is that persevering in anything shapes us as well as the world around us.

Persistent prayer shapes our character, reinforces our tenacity, focuses our trust on the Lord, and increases our capacity to carry the authority and anointing that the Father has given us. At Jesus Culture, we know that the increase in authority and anointing for healing that we have seen is directly related to sustained prayer.

FOUR KEYS TO SUSTAIN PRAYER

How do you sustain prayer? If you have tried to abide in prayer for very long, you know that there is a reason Jesus mentioned the possibility of losing heart. There are plenty of ways and plenty of reasons to become weary, frustrated, or disappointed and give up praying. You can persist in prayer for only so long on human zeal and effort alone. If you start praying because you feel guilty or because of a conviction that you have to, it won't last long. A disciplined life, as important as that is, will get you only so far if you are going to give yourself to sustained prayer. During our "Summer of Prayer," we knew we needed to pray until we obtained what we were asking for, yet we knew we couldn't just "work harder" for it. Striving harder sounded like a recipe for burnout. So how were we to sustain prayer?

Four things, I believe, are needed to sustain prayer. There are probably more, but these are the four things the Lord taught us to help us persevere in pursuing Him and praying for our city. The first is *intimacy*. The life of a believer is to be led by loving God and being loved by Him. Everything must flow from this. Andrew Murray, in sharing his secrets of prayer, stresses the importance of intimacy with the Father. "(Jesus) wants us to see that the secret of effective prayer is to have the heart filled with the Father-love of God."[20] Therefore, "The knowledge of God's Father-love is the first and simplest, but also the last and highest lesson in the school of prayer."[21] Anything that is not motivated by our love for God is unstable. Intimacy enables us to sustain prayer because it makes prayer a matter of spending time with the One you love, which is the natural expression and desire of love. Prayer is hard to sustain if your view of God is anything but that of a loving Father. Many people view God as someone who is angry, sad, or disappointed with them. Who wants to hang out in prayer for a few hours with a God who is just going to let them know He isn't pleased with them? Nobody. Intimacy changes any misconceptions you might have about God, because it brings you face to face with Him—a good Daddy. It's easy to sustain prayer with a God who is so extravagantly in love with you and is always telling you about it.

When our view of Father God comes into focus, we discover that His desire for His sons and daughters is not that we would be His servants but His friends and partners. A lot of believers still need to make this move from being employees in prayer to friends in prayer. When I was nineteen years old, I worked for a short time on a painting crew. I was the grunt who had to do all the jobs nobody else wanted to do. It was brutal. I hated it. But here's the crazy thing. If one of my friends asks me to come over and paint his house with him, I do it with joy. I might be imitating the exact same job I did at nineteen, but it is completely different when I am working alongside my friend because I am not his employee; I am his friend, and we are accomplishing a task together. I don't *have* to; I *get* to. We *get* to pray with our Friend Jesus. The Head Intercessor who lives to make intercession for us has invited us in to join with Him as He intercedes. Can you think of anything better than partnering with Jesus to see the dreams of His heart realized? Intimacy must be at the core of your prayer life, or it will either be short-lived or a nagging duty.

The second key to sustain prayer is *responsibility*. Many people don't sustain prayer for their city because they don't feel any responsibility for their region. If you live with a sense of responsibility, you will live differently. Let me give you an example. I have three gorgeous kids! As a dad, I have the privilege of responding to late-night calls and cries. It might be a bad dream. It might be a request for water. It might be that they just decided to wake up at three in the morning. Whatever the reason is, when they call I'm up and in their rooms seeing what I can do for them. They are my children, and I have a responsibility to be aware of their needs and listen for their cries. However, if I were to stay the night at one of my friend's houses, things would be different. If I woke up to the cries of my friend's children in the middle of the night, I would more than likely find earplugs, roll over, and go back to sleep. Why? Because those children aren't my responsibility. I know my friend will do his "Daddy role" and get up to check out what is going on. I respond differently to their needs than to my own children's needs.

It is the same with your city. If you don't take responsibility for your city or campus or workplace and the people in it, then when something happens you will roll over and fall back to sleep instead of going to prayer. You don't disengage because your heart is evil but because those aren't your kids. You haven't taken responsibility for your city. People sustain prayer for things they feel responsible for. Many people have a hard time upholding prayer because they have no real sense of responsibility for their city or their nation.

Second Kings 4 tells of an interaction Elisha had with a widow. The creditor was coming to take her two sons to be his slaves because of the debt left behind by her husband, so the widow cried out to Elisha to intervene. Partnering with the widow, Elisha supernaturally provided the resources needed to pay off the creditor and save her sons. What I want you to catch is that the widow's cry was birthed out of a sense of responsibility for her sons. She lifted up her voice because her sons were headed into slavery. We also must lift up our voice in a cry to Heaven for those around us whose lives are being taken captive.

If you have ever been to TheCall, you have encountered a company of people who have taken responsibility for their nation.[22] At TheCall, people stand for twelve hours before the Lord, fasting and praying, often with the sun beating down on them or the rain falling. They aren't there just to be intimate with the Lord; they are there to cry out for their nation, of which they have taken ownership. It's not okay to sit back while unjust laws are passed, violence increases, babies are aborted, people live in poverty, and racism still exists in our nations. These issues must drive us to prayer as we take responsibility for our nations and call out for a great outpouring of the Holy Spirit to see them turn back to God.

The third key to sustained prayer is a *"theology of breakthrough."* Mike Bickle coined this phrase when describing one of their keys to sustaining prayer at the International House of Prayer. Put simply, you've got to believe God is going to show up when you pray. Again, Andrew Murray advises in the ways of prayer: "We may and must confidently expect an answer to our prayer."[23] Many people, without realizing, go through the motions of prayer with no power because they don't really believe their prayers move the heart of God. But the truth is that we have a God who is even more eager to show up in our city than we are for Him to show up! Isaiah 64:4 says that God acts for those who wait for Him. That means God is moved to action on behalf of those who seek Him in prayer. Sustaining prayer isn't so arduous when you believe God responds to your prayer. You trust that breakthrough will come because God answers prayer. Our faith is not in our ability to pray but in His ability to answer. It may take a while. It may seem like God is slow. But He will answer because you are praying. Your ability to continue praying when it seems that God is not listening directly relates to your knowledge of His character. George Mueller, when asked if he had any unanswered prayers, confidently replied, "No. That is except for one. But it will be. How can it be any other way? I am still praying."[24] The unanswered prayer was for the conversion of a friend's son. At Mueller's funeral, that son gave his life to Jesus. Mueller was a man confident in the character of God and confident in the effect his prayers had to move Heaven.

The fourth key to sustained prayer is *prophetic revelation*. This has been a huge influence in our ministry. When the Lord speaks to us through dreams, prophetic words, Scriptures, and other prophetic experiences, He's providing fuel for our fires of prayer. These things give direction and let us know we are on the right track. Any time we begin to feel weary in our prayers, the Lord is faithful and sends us a dream or a prophetic word or enlivens a Scripture for us, and faith to keep pressing in ignites again in our hearts. It is one of the most exciting, dynamic aspects of our interactions with the Lord. It makes prayer an adventure.

Beyond learning to *receive* prophetic revelation, we've had to learn how to *carry* prophetic revelation. It is one thing to hear a prophetic word; it is a whole other thing to carry that prophetic word in prayer. At Jesus Culture, we have great value for the prophetic and have made it our practice to bring prophetic words back to the Lord in prayer consistently. I have pages and pages of prophetic words that have become fuel for my prayer life. I have words that I received in my teenage years. I am always going back to them, reviewing them, and praying through them as I remind myself, and the Lord, of what He said. I heard a preacher say once, "Prayer is really just us finding out what God wants to do and then going back to Him and asking Him to do that." Through prophetic revelation, the Lord draws our focus to what He is doing so we can hit the mark in prayer. Our faith to pray is greatly augmented when we know we are in agreement with the Lord on a particular issue.

ENDNOTES

1. Frank Bartleman, *Another Wave of Revival* (New York: Whitaker House, 1982), 14.

2. Ibid., 28.

3. Murray, *With Christ in the School of Prayer*, 44.

4. Bounds, *Power Through Prayer*, 13.

5. Murray, *With Christ in the School of Prayer*, 28.

6. Ibid., 25.

7. Wallis, *In the Day of Thy Power*, 85.

8. Bounds, *Power Through Prayer*, 44.

9. Ibid., 45.

10. J.E. Orr, *The Flaming Tongue* (Chicago, IL: Moody Press, 1973), 15.

11. Solomon B. Shaw, *The Great Revival in Wales* (New York, NY: Christian Life Books, 2002), 76.

12. Warren W. Harkins, *I Saw the Welsh Revival* (Pensacola, FL: Christian Life Books, 2002), 31.

13. Buckingham, *Daughter of Destiny*, 146.

14. Ibid., 147.

15. Bounds, *Power Through Prayer*, 29.

16. Buckingham, *Daughter of Destiny*, 147.

17. Bill Johnson, "Here are those quotes."

18. "Shasta Dam, California," Bureau of Reclamation Homepage, Statistics, http://www.usbr.gov/dataweb/dams/ca10186.htm (accessed April 20, 2009).

19. Murray, *With Christ in the School of Prayer,* 10.

20. Ibid., 48.

21. Ibid., 31.

22. For more information visit: http://www.thecall.com/.

23. Murray, *With Christ in the School of Prayer*, 39.

24. I have heard Bill Johnson many times tell the story about the missionary George Mueller.

WHEN HEAVEN BREAKS OUT

In the previous section, we reviewed four keys that will help effectively sustain revival prayer. If we were to add a fifth, perhaps it would be the illustration of testimonies recorded in history. The written record of what God has done through ordinary people confronts us with what is possible and available to the yielded vessel.

In his book, *The Glory Within*, prayer leader, Corey Russell, invites readers to experience the Holy Spirit in a deeper way. Even though his book focuses uniquely on the language of the Spirit—praying in tongues—the underlying theme is a call for men and women to press in to encounter more of God. Even for those who have tasted the "Pentecostal" experience by receiving the "baptism of the Holy Spirit," there is still more. Unfortunately, even people in Spirit-filled communities can stall at certain landmark moments in their relationship with God. For many, it is their first taste of Holy Spirit baptism, with the dynamic manifestation of speaking in tongues. This brings such refreshing and delight that it becomes difficult for their minds to wrap around the notion of anything beyond that. And yet, there is still more...

The early church was filled with the Spirit and filled again. Paul never used prohibited language when discussing the filling of the Spirit. Quite the opposite. He instructed: "be filled with the Spirit" (Eph. 5:18). When translated properly, this phrase literally means to keep on being filled with the Spirit.

The disciples were filled when Jesus breathed upon them in John 20. Many theologians would consider this a "filling unto salvation," where they were actually born again by the Spirit. Then, of course, there is the famous Day of Pentecost outpouring where the 120 in the upper room were filled with the Holy Spirit and spoke in other tongues. In this scenario, they were stepping into a fulfilled prophecy, as Jesus pointed to a subsequent experience where they would be "endued with power from on high" (Luke 24:49, KJV). After this, the book of Acts records multiple other fillings, both individually and corporately. While these biblical testimonies are compelling, we see the same patterns in the lives of contemporary revivalists.

In this chapter from *The Glory Within*, Corey introduces readers to John G. Lake. While he is notable for his missionary efforts in South Africa and ministry of divine healing, perhaps his greatest legacy is his relationship with and pursuit of the Holy Spirit. Allow the following testimony about John G. Lake to be a prophetic invitation for you to cry out for the same encounter with the "more" of God in your own life.

For us to ask for more revival rain, we need to take the limits off how much rain we believe is available. It's more than a one-time experience at an altar or during a prayer meeting. It's greater than speaking in tongues or giving a word of prophecy. While both of those manifestations are important, they do not contain the fullness of the One called Holy Spirit.

CHAPTER 9

THERE IS MORE

Corey Russell

About ten years ago I was gripped with the subject of the baptism of the Holy Spirit. I had already received the personal, devotional gift of tongues, and my life was filled with many other blessings and gifts of the Spirit. But deep within my heart, I knew that there had to be more. I was desperate for all that God would give to a human soul, and I knew that the "all" was more than the small manifestations of the gifts that I saw in my own life and the lives of those around me.

I read the book of Acts, I read biographies of the great heroes of the faith, but it was only when I stumbled across the writings of John G. Lake—one of the fathers of the Pentecostal movement—that I began to find language for the cry of my heart. As I read his sermons, I discovered that the subject of the baptism of the Spirit and its impact on the Christian life has been greatly reduced over the last decades in the Church. We have treated this subject so lightly, yet this is the holiest thing that God can give to the human soul. Jesus suffered death on the cross, fought and defeated all the powers of hell, and finally ascended into Heaven and received the Spirit from the Father so that He could pour it out on us; He understood the value of this gift.

On the Day of Pentecost, one hundred and twenty believers were baptized in the Holy Spirit and they turned the world upside down. Today, the Church has millions of believers who are "baptized in the Spirit," and yet there is very little difference between them and the world. We have fallen so far short in our understanding of the baptism of the Spirit and what God longs to do in the souls of people. We cannot continue to believe that we possess all that God intended because we speak in tongues occasionally and have had a few experiences with manifestations of the Spirit. Simply reading the New Testament should convince us that there is a fundamental breakdown between what Jesus promised (and the early Church experienced) and what we experience today.

John G. Lake

I want to spend some time looking at the writings of John G. Lake. Lake arguably walked in some of the greatest levels of spiritual authority and power seen since the early Church. In his initial eighteen months as a missionary in South Africa, Lake planted over one hundred churches. At the end of his five years of ministry in that nation, he left behind 1250 preachers, 625 congregations, over 100,000 new converts, and countless testimonies of miraculous healings.[1] He then moved back to the United States—to Spokane, Washington—and set up a ministry school of healing. In its initial five years of existence, that school documented and recorded over 100,000 healings. The government actually investigated what had become known as the Healing Rooms, and gave this report: *"Rev. Lake, through divine healing, has made Spokane the healthiest city in the world, according to United States' statistics."*[2] Here is an example of the power that Lake and his students were accustomed to seeing:

Mrs. Constance Hoag, Puyallup, Washington, broke her kneecap. A section of the bone protruded through the flesh. She wrote requesting that ministers of the Healing Rooms lay their hands upon a handkerchief in faith and prayer and send it to her, in accordance with Acts 19:12. This was done. She applied the handkerchief to the knee and in about 15 minutes the pain had gone, and in an hour the bone had returned to place. A few days later she visited Spokane—well.[3]

This servant of God taught more on the baptism of the Holy Spirit than on any other subject. His own life was marked by an overwhelming desire to experience the fullness of the baptism of the Spirit, and his testimony of how God answered that hunger is powerful and provoking. John G. Lake was born in 1870. He was saved during his teenage years and began a successful ministry of healing in his 20s. This ministry continued for ten years, and Lake saw hundreds of people saved and healed. In a sermon delivered in 1921, Lake described that period of time and his hunger for more of the Holy Spirit:

> I ministered for ten years in the power of God. Hundreds and hundreds of people were healed by the power of God during this ten years, and I could feel the conscious flow of the Holy Spirit through my soul and my hands.

> But at the end of that ten years I believe I was the hungriest man for God that ever lived. There was such a hunger for God that as I left my offices in Chicago and walked down the street, my soul would break out, and I would cry, "Oh God!" I have had people stop and look at me in wonder. It was the yearning passion of my soul, asking for God in a greater measure than I then knew. But my friends would say: "Mr. Lake, you have a beautiful baptism in the Holy Ghost." Yes, it was nice as far as it went, but it was not answering the cry of my heart. I was growing up into a

larger understanding of God and my own soul's need. My soul was demanding a greater entrance into God, His love, Presence and power.[4]

Lake began to earnestly fast and pray and cry out for the baptism of the Spirit. He spent nine months in intense intercession, begging God to baptize him in the way that Jesus's disciples had been baptized. One afternoon, a friend invited him to come and visit a woman who was suffering from severe rheumatism. While the friend conversed with the woman, Lake sat in a chair in the corner, crying out to God deep within his soul. Suddenly he was aware of the Presence of God surrounding him, and he heard the Lord say, "I have heard your prayers, I have seen your tears. You are now baptized in the Holy Spirit."[5] At that moment, what felt like volts of electricity began to surge through his body. When he stretched out his hand toward the woman, his friend was thrown to the floor by the power released, and she was instantly healed and arose from her wheelchair. At this, his friend cried out, "Praise the Lord, John, Jesus has baptized you in the Holy Ghost!"[6]

It is true that after this encounter there was an increase in the anointing on Lake's ministry, especially in the realm of healing. He went through a season where he was able, simply by laying hands on a person, to tell which organ was diseased and how severely it was affected. He visited hospitals and accurately diagnosed numerous patients that the doctors had given up on. Power was definitely a part of this baptism of the Spirit! But it was only a part. I want to share some of Lake's own writings related to the baptism of the Spirit. More than any other man in recent Church history, he grasped the heart of God behind the Day of Pentecost, and said *yes* to the highest vision of the Christian life.

> The outpouring of the Holy Ghost is the greatest event in Christian history—greater than the crucifixion, of greater import than the resurrection, greater than the ascension,

greater than the glorification. It was the end and finality which the crucifixion, resurrection, and glorification sought to accomplish.

If Jesus Christ had been crucified and there had been no resurrection, His death on the cross would have been without avail, insofar as the salvation of mankind is concerned. Or if He had risen from the grave in resurrection, failed to reach the throne of God and receive from the Father the gift of the Holy Ghost, the purpose for which He died and for which He arose would have been missed.

There was no failure! Jesus went to the ultimate, the very throne and heart of God, and secured right out of the heavenly treasury the Almighty Spirit and poured Him forth upon the world in divine baptism; that is why we are here!

...in order to obtain this gift, Jesus Christ lived in the world, bled on the cross, entered into the darkness of death and hell and the grave, grappled with and strangled that accursed power, came forth again, and finally ascended to heaven in order to secure it for you and me. If there is anything under heaven that ought to command our reverence, our Holy reverence, our reverence beyond anything else in the world, it surely is the subject of the Baptism of the Holy Ghost.[7]

Will you speak in tongues when you are baptized in the Holy Ghost? Yes, you will, but you will do an awful lot more than that, bless God. An awful lot more than that! You will speak with the soul of Jesus Christ. You will feel with the heart of the Son of God. Your heart will beat with a heavenly desire to bless the world, because it is the pulse of Jesus that is throbbing in your soul.[8]

Jesus went to heaven in order that the very treasury of the heart of the eternal God might be unlocked for your benefit, and that out of the very soul of the eternal God, the streams of His life and nature would possess you from the crown of your head to the soles of your feet, and that there would be just as much of the eternal God in your toenails and in your brain as each are capable of containing. In other words, from the very soles of your feet to the last hair on the top of your head, every cell of your being, would be a residence of the Spirit of the living God. Man is made alive by God and with God, by the Spirit.[9]

The greatest manifestation of the Holy Ghost baptized life ever given to the world was not in the preaching of the apostles, it was not in the wonderful manifestations of God that took place at their hands, it was in the unselfishness manifested by the church. Think of it! Three thousand Holy Ghost baptized Christians in Jerusalem from the day of Pentecost onward who loved their neighbor's children as much as their own, who were so anxious for fear their brethren did not have enough to eat, that they sold their estates, and brought the money and laid it at the apostle's feet, and said: "Distribute it, carry the glow and the fire and the wonder of this divine salvation to the whole world." That showed what God had wrought in their hearts. Oh, I wish we could arrive at that place where this church was baptized in that degree of unselfishness.[10]

What Lake understood was that the baptism of the Spirit is about the fullness of God. We were created for communion; we were made to contain the glory of God. At salvation He places His Spirit in us, but when we are baptized, the Spirit that lives in us consumes us. We are immersed in who God is, and we manifest His life at every level: His power, His authority, and His sacrificial love. That is actually what it means to be baptized: total immersion. The baptism of the

Spirit takes the reality of the life of God within and makes that reality experientially known to every part of our beings—body, soul, and spirit. Lake says it this way:

> ...beloved, we have not comprehended the greatness of God's intent. Not that we have not received the Spirit, but our lives have not been sufficiently surrendered to God. We must keep ascending right to the throne, right into the heart of God, right into the soul of the Glorified.[11]

This is the difference between the reality of the Holy Spirit *in* us and the Holy Spirit *upon* us. Again and again, Scripture testifies that there is more; there is a baptism of the Holy Spirit available to all believers. In fact, I believe that there are multiple baptisms. There are fresh encounters with the life of God that are released over the course of every believer's life. If you look at the New Testament Church and the lives of the disciples, it seems clear that there are multiple waves of anointing, power, and life that are received and experienced. As believers, we are invited to receive more and more of the Holy Spirit. *We are being baptized deeper into a Person, immersed in His life, His love, and His power.*

Reading the sermons of John G. Lake destroyed my spiritual complacency and I became consumed with desire for the fullness of all that God is willing to give His children. I am grateful for the baptism of the Spirit that I have received; I am grateful for the way that speaking in tongues has transformed my life—purifying my heart and mind, releasing revelation, strengthening my spirit, and overthrowing the schemes of the enemy—but I believe that there is more. As we engage the Holy Spirit through tongues and continue to press in for more, the Lord will usher us into greater measures of the fullness of God and the gifts of the Spirit. I believe that tongues is a gateway gift. The greatest signs and wonders, the most powerful healing and deliverance ministries, and the greatest harvest of souls will be released as the end-time Church reaps the fruit of ceaseless prayer in the Spirit.

ENDNOTES

1. *John G. Lake: His Life, His Sermons, His Boldness of Faith* (Fort Worth, TX: Kenneth Copeland Publications, 1994), xxv-xxvii.

2. Ibid., xxx.

3. Ibid., 320.

4. John G. Lake, "The Baptism of the Holy Ghost," in *John G. Lake: His Life, His Sermons, His Boldness of Faith* (Fort Worth, TX: Kenneth Copeland Publications, 1994), 483.

5. Gordon Lindsay, *John G. Lake: Apostle to Africa* (Dallas, TX: Christ For the Nations, Inc., 1987), 18.

6. Ibid., 19.

7. John G. Lake, "The Baptism of the Holy Ghost," in *John G. Lake: His Life, His Sermons, His Boldness of Faith* (Fort Worth, TX: Kenneth Copeland Publications, 1994), 476.

8. Ibid., 484.

9. Ibid., 480.

10. Ibid., 490.

11. Ibid., 480.

This compilation has been intentional, taking you on a journey from the cry of revival to prayer for revival to the quest for increased revival. This is where we are right now. God is moving. It's raining. The Holy Spirit is breaking out in places all across the world. The great need of the hour is to keep our hands off His activity, while investing our efforts and energies to steward Heaven's movement on earth. As we steward the Spirit's movement, we will in turn witness increased revival and outpouring.

What does increased revival look like? A greater agreement between what the New Testament Church looked like and what the contemporary church looks like. This has nothing to do with aesthetics—music, technology, art, dance, projector screens, etc. The integration of modern techniques is not inherently positive or negative. If being edgy trumps anointing, the "edge" becomes negative. However, if our desire is to seize technology to help steward His Presence in a greater, more effective way, the effort is positive. A return to the New Testament model is not about abandoning contemporary music or the use of technology; it is about identifying the early church's emphasis and restoring that to a place of priority.

Above all, the emphasis of the early church was a Person: Holy Spirit. He was not contained or restrained by religious methods; He was everything. In fact, the early church existed to accommodate the movement of Holy Spirit. In the following chapter, I have explored some unique biblical imagery from Second Samuel 6 that specifically addresses what happens when man tries to contain the Presence of God. The sad result is that people, churches and entire movements are dying right beside the possibility of historic outpouring. God is extending His invitation for them to participate in His movement on earth. Sadly, many choose safety and comfort over the unknown, unexplored places of revival. Now, since God is Sovereign King, He will ensure that His Kingdom comes to earth. Period. We can safely plan on that. At the same time, I do not want us to miss the opportunity to partner with God in ushering in historic, end-time revival. I am quite convinced He has been extending this opportunity to people and communities throughout the ages—only a few have said *yes* to His invitation.

I included the following chapter from the book *The Fire That Never Sleeps,* since the objective of that work was to give people strategies on sustaining revival. Although this is a confrontational chapter, it is absolutely necessary if we want to experience everything we have read about so far on a sustained basis. God is moving. The fact is undeniable. The question is: How will we respond to His movement? Will we reject it? Tolerate it? Or actually celebrate it, welcoming the Spirit's supernatural activity with open arms?

CHAPTER 10

DON'T DIE BESIDE THE ARK

Larry Sparks

> *If they wait to see a work of God without difficulties*
> *and stumbling-blocks, it will be like the fool's*
> *waiting at the river side to have the water all run*
> *by. A work of God without stumbling-blocks is*
> *never to be expected.... There never yet was any*
> *great manifestation that God made of himself to the*
> *world, without many difficulties attending it.*
> —JONATHAN EDWARDS

God is looking for a people who are ready to accommodate a visitation of His glory in their midst—*no matter what it costs.* Popularity. Prominence. Power. Notoriety. Reputation. When we measure these things beside the possibility of experiencing a visitation of God's Presence, they must all fall miserably short. This is essential in order for our prayers for revival to prevail.

A New Demonstration of Christianity

I want us to consider some of the things that prevent us from going full force after revival in our lives and churches. There is no room for halfhearted effort when it comes to our desperate cry for the move of God. When I say *desperate* or use the term *desperation*, I am not implying that we are trying to twist God's arm or coerce Him to send an outpouring of the Spirit. Desperation does not seek to change God from being unwilling to willing. He is not clenching His fist around revival, looking to send it down to the person who begs, barters, and pleads long enough. Not at all. Rather, it's desperation to align our hearts with the Father's. This prayer is not about begging God to open Heaven. Instead, it is asking the Holy Spirit to help us steward the open Heaven we have already received because of Pentecost.

God not only wants to send revival; He wants us to receive the invitation that revival extends, make the appropriate adjustments, and live out a whole new expression of Christianity. This is what the world is in dire need of. Revivalist Leonard Ravenhill said it best: "the world outside there is not waiting for a new definition of Christianity, it's waiting for a new demonstration of Christianity."

If we desire for our homes, churches, communities, and nations to live under an open Heaven, we must pray like there is nothing more important to us than welcoming the move of God with open arms.

Compromise That Unplugs Our Prayers

When we compromise on our definition of revival, we are essential pulling the plug on our prayers. We are removing them from their power source. To pray with effectiveness, there must be an element of strong belief. We might claim to have faith for revival, but ultimately it is revival with strings attached. This will not suffice.

The compromise I am specifically addressing is the desire to have a people-pleasing revival. This is historically and fundamentally impossible. We can use all the revival language we want in our services, books, and conferences. We can hold all-night revival prayer meetings. No matter how intense our efforts, if ultimately we have an agenda in our heart to "steady the ox cart," we are not fit to host God's glory. Consider this account in Scripture for a moment:

> *And David and all the house of Israel were celebrating before the Lord, with songs and lyres and harps and tambourines and castanets and cymbals. And when they came to the threshing floor of Nacon, Uzzah put out his hand to the ark of God and took hold of it, for the oxen stumbled. And the anger of the Lord was kindled against Uzzah, and God struck him down there because of his error, and he died there beside the ark of God* (2 Samuel 6:5-7).

In Second Samuel 6:5–7, we see what happens when man makes any attempt to "steady" the Presence of God. Everything was set for the day to be glorious. The Ark of the Covenant had been recaptured from the Philistines, and now there was a great procession heralding the return of God's Presence among the people. For our purposes, it is worth noting that Uzzah's sin was taking hold of the Ark when the ox stumbled (see v. 6). The Message Bible translates verse 7 in an interesting way, perhaps bringing more clarity to the severity of God's judgment upon Uzzah. We read that *"God blazed in anger against Uzzah and struck him hard because he had profaned the Chest."*

When it comes to Old Testament accounts like this, we cannot assume to draw prophetic parallels between this story and New Testament realities. While these passages may not be prophetic in nature, I am convinced they are illustrative. They reveal a powerful principle about God's Presence and humankind's stewardship. God is God. He moves on His own terms. Yes, He involves us. Yes, we are co-laborers with Him and joint-heirs with Christ. Yes, we are friends of God. This is all true. But at the day's end, we must weigh all these realities in light of the fact that God is God. He is God Almighty, who inhabits eternity (see Isa. 57:15). I want whatever *He* wants. His definition of revival must be mine; otherwise I will be tempted to adjust what He is doing to suit my preferences. This is happening across the earth today. Since Pentecost, the Holy Spirit has been poured out. We have a choice to make: Will we embrace this outpouring on God's terms, or will we try to "steady the cart" and adapt what God is doing to accommodate our systems?

WHAT KILLS REVIVAL?

Revival dies for a number of reasons. One of the main ones is humankind's poor stewardship of the Holy Spirit's activity. In fact, this is the reason many people do not experience the true fire of revival to begin with. The Holy Spirit broods over a community, church, or region looking for the man or woman who will say what God is saying and embrace what He is doing. We see this perfectly illustrated in the Creation account in Genesis 1.

In Genesis 1:2, we note that "the Spirit of God was hovering over the face of the waters." He was present, but He only moved in creative power when the word of the Lord was spoken. This is how the Trinity operates—in complete and absolute unity. The Spirit does whatever the Father declares. They are absolutely in sync with one another. In revival, the Spirit moves wherever there are people who are thinking, saying, and moving in alignment with the Father. This is not some call to perfectionism. The Spirit doesn't require our perfect performance to work with; He simply needs willingness to yield to whatever the Father wants to do. This is not to say character is unimportant. Quite the contrary: Christ-like character is imperative to sustaining a Christ-like anointing in revival. The fact is, God uses ordinary, broken, humble people to accomplish His purposes. In being such yielded vessels, we will not dare try to touch what God is doing. Even if we don't fully understand everything that comes with revival, we will celebrate the Spirit's Presence in our midst rather than shutting down what we consider uncomfortable.

Again, Second Samuel 6 illustrates how serious it is for us to keep our hands off a move of God's Spirit. Yes, we pastor it. Of course, church leaders need to assume a stewardship in a season of outpouring. At the same time, we cannot cry out for revival on our terms and conditions. Do you know what we will get? Nothing.

Or worse, the Spirit of God may noticeably move in our community, and immediately we make decisions that shut down His activity. *God looks to see how His people will respond to the move of His Presence.* Will we embrace revival and everything that comes with it, or will we be like Uzzah and try to *steady the cart.* This language so vividly captures how many feel when the Holy Spirit begins to move. It is uncomfortable. People respond unusually. There are often dramatic manifestations as the Holy Spirit touches people and convicts their hearts. Because these things are so foreign to us, we get nervous and immediately look for some "big red button" to press that will shut everything down. We want revival without the mess. This is impossible.

This is not to say that we embrace disorder and chaos. Certainly not. However, we must consider revival so precious, so priceless that we are willing to take the bad with the good, and learn how to navigate through the bad.

ARE WE OUT OF ORDER?

Continuing on this subject of order and disorder in revival, we would do well to carefully review what the apostle Paul considered to be *order.*

Many cite First Corinthians 14:40, where Paul reminds the church in Corinth that "all things should be done decently and in order." Absolutely. Here is my question: What does order look like from Paul's context? Verse 40 is the concluding passage in an entire chapter about the operation of spiritual gifts in a corporate gathering—namely the two more controversial manifestations of tongues and prophecy.

Paul's paradigm of "decently and in order" was not the complete absence of supernatural activity in corporate gatherings or in our Christian lives. Far from it. He was not urging the Corinthians to shut down the move of the Spirit, but rather to pastor and steward it. He was not even telling them to "take it outside," as many do today. Many of us believe in the move of the Spirit theologically, but when it comes to the *expression* of His Presence and power, we encourage people to keep *that Holy Spirit stuff* in their small groups, or we schedule "renewal services" at times when no one could possibly attend the meetings, certain that we do not frighten people away. I don't want our false idea of decently and in order to deceive us right out of an encounter with the glory of God. It's Scriptural language we use to justify our desire to be in control—to regulate the untamable Spirit of God. Truth be told, the Bible never tells us that the Holy Spirit is a gentleman. But one thing is for sure: He is the ultimate personification of good. Let's put it this way: if Jesus considered the Holy Spirit to be the best gift imaginable (see Luke 11:13), then we are safe to trust in His ways.

The question we must always ask is *what is the fruit*? If Jesus is being exalted and souls are being genuinely saved, we must recognize the Presence of the Holy Spirit in the midst of what we might find chaotic, confusing, and outside of our comfort zones. If lives are radically transformed by a supernatural touch of God's power, it does not matter what kind of "package" the encounter comes in. If someone ends up laughing hysterically, lying prostrate on the floor for hours, shaking, crying, or shouting, we have no right to judge. These are simply evidences of the human flesh responding to the supernatural touch of God's Presence. We do not evaluate the genuineness of revival by manifestations; we evaluate by life transformation. If people's encounters with God—however odd or unusual—serve as launching pads for living transformed lifestyles, we should celebrate, not scrutinize.

WHEN HOLY CHAOS BREAKS OUT

What may appear like chaos to us in the twenty-first century church might be complete order to God. When we read testimonies of the great revivals of old, we often witness a holy pandemonium breaking out. Consider how George Whitefield describes one instance of his preaching the Gospel in Edinburgh, Scotland, in 1742:

> Such a commotion was surely never heard of, especially about eleven o'clock at night. It far outdid anything I ever saw in America. For about an hour and a half there was such weeping, so many felling into deep distress, and manifest it in various ways, that description is impossible. The people seemed to be smitten in scores. They were carried off and brought into the house like wounded soldiers taken from a field of battle. Their agonies and cries were deeply effecting.[1]

Christians from various traditions and multiple denominations celebrate the evangelistic efforts of Whitefield, recognizing him as a vital spokesman for spiritual awakening. Yet when we review specific instances where he preached the Gospel and witnessed mass conversions, we continually read of "disorderly" scenes such as the one above.

Let us move on to John Wesley, the founder of Methodism and a great pioneer for itinerant evangelism. He often preached to over five thousand people during his 7:00 a.m. Sunday morning service. Revival historian Wesley Duewel describes the scene of Wesley's church service in the following terms:

> Well-dressed, mature people suddenly cried out as if in the agonies of death. Both men and women, outside and

inside the church buildings, would tremble and sink to the ground.[2]

It is impossible for us to cry out for revival, as in the days of old, and then be disappointed when the days-of-old manifestations start happening. Again, God has a higher concept of "decently and in order" than we do. Don't be surprised if what seems foolish at first glance is the very power of God moving in your midst, bringing healing, deliverance, and salvation.

WHEN WE DIE NEXT TO REVIVAL

This brings us back to Second Samuel 6, where Uzzah tries to steady the Ark. When we try to steady the move of God, we run the risk of missing revival, thus dying to the glorious things God has planned for our lives, churches, cities, and so on. As a result of Uzzah's sin, he died. Scripture does not reveal anything about Uzzah's intentions for steadying the Ark; nor should we draw meaning when such is not clearly revealed. All we know is what he did and the dramatic consequence.

Here is what we do see: God makes a very clear point about His Presence and humanity's tendency to want to control it. If we truly desire the life and visitation of revival, we will align ourselves with what God is doing rather than manipulate His work to fit our vision of Christianity. Revival is the unceasing mercy of God, sovereignly reaching out to humankind and calling us to embrace *His* definition of what the Christian life looks like. This is why revival is often so confrontational. It confronts apathy and complacency, for sure.

God will not send revival to those who have an agenda to control His activity and movement. In fact, many communities *die* beside the Ark of God. What does this mean? The Holy Spirit wants to move powerfully, but due to tradition, religion, desire to please people, the fear of man—a number of factors—we reject

God's invitation for revival. As a result, we say a costly "no" to the move of His Spirit, continue on with spiritual "business as usual," and, sadly, die *right beside* the possibility of tremendous outpouring. The Spirit is willing; it is we who tell Him no, or "I want it on my terms," or "I want it *this way.*"

When all is said and done, we must be ready to answer this pivotal question: Whom do I want to make comfortable with my life or in my church—God or man? How we answer this determines whether we are qualified for the outpouring of revival. This determines everything.

ENDNOTES

1. Albert D. Belden, *George Whitefield—The Awakener* (London: Sampson Low), 65.

2. Wesley Duewel, *Revival Fires* (Grand Rapids: Zondervan, 1995), 77.

When I consider some of the contemporary pioneers of revival, Don Nori Sr. comes straight to mind. Revivalists come in a variety of expressions. They aren't always evangelists, teachers or pastors. They aren't always the ones speaking on stage. Sometimes, they are the ones called to come alongside others and help amplify their prophetic voices.

In 1983, Pastor Don (as he is affectionately called) was summoned by the Lord through a supernatural visitation to birth what would become Destiny Image Publishers. Even though I currently serve as publisher for this wonderful publishing house, I am not stretching the truth in the least by saying these landmark books have been responsible for shaping my Christian life for over fifteen years. Long before I ever dreamed of working for the company, let alone considering ministry or publishing as a career path, books like *God Chasers* and *When Heaven Invades Earth* introduced me to a new vision of the Christian faith. These messages and messengers birthed a hunger within my heart to pursue the "more" of God. I'm grateful to say that I've been on pursuit ever since.

Don's writing comes from a place of brokenness, transparency, and deep intimacy with God. He is a true prophet who is constantly looking for what the Father is doing and listening for what He is saying. For revival to break out in our lives, churches, and communities, we must be willing to live outside of the "box." After all, God Almighty cannot be contained to any box we attempt to place Him in—be it the box of religion, traditionalism, liturgy, etc. Anything that places a ceiling on our quest for God must be removed. In this segment from his book *God: Out of Control, Out of the Box, Out of Time,* Pastor Don provides a blueprint for how we should embrace God's revival activity in our lives and churches. Will it be uncomfortable? Sure. Will the Spirit's movement in our midst upset how things have "always been done"? Undoubtedly. Is the manifestation and habitation of His Presence worth it?

Always...

CHAPTER 11

LIVING OUT OF YOUR BOX

Don Nori Sr.

Not being able to fully understand God is frustrating,
but it is ridiculous for us to think we have the
right to limit God to something we are capable of
comprehending. What a stunted, insignificant god
that would be! If my mind is the size of a soda can and
God is the size of all the oceans, it would be stupid
for me to say He is only the small amount of water I
can scoop into my little can. God is so much bigger.
—FRANCIS CHAN

The Holy Spirit often wants to do things different from our order of church service, our order of worship, our order of life.

God is showing Himself in a powerful way. God is coming into our churches and He won't care what is in His way—procedures, policies, programs—He will be out of control.

Be careful that you are not holding on to the wrong thing, because if you are, you will go down with the religious system He is dismantling. There is nothing sacred in our buildings, there is nothing sacred in our order of service or in how we worship. The only sacred thing is *His manifest Presence.*

His Manifest Presence

When His manifest Presence is evidenced in the church, not much else matters. When God is in the house, all the focus is on Him.

I was in Kentucky for meetings. I was supposed to teach six times to various audiences. The first morning, I taught the pastors to get ready for God to move in. I remember telling them, "When God is in the house, you don't even have to preach." *Not preach? Will we backslide? Will the people be confused?* they wondered. I responded to their questions by telling them again to "Get ready!" Little did I know that very night the Presence of God would explode into that same auditorium.

That evening, His Presence was so mighty that there was never one word spoken from the microphone. No one said, "Welcome to the service." No one said, "Don Nori is here." No one took an offering. No one led worship—but the worship of the Lord arose in the building. I looked at the pastor and he could hardly stand up.

I said, "Pastor, I don't think I should preach tonight."

He looked at me and said, "You're not preaching tonight?"

I said, "Pastor, when the Man is in the house, this man has got nothing to say."

We watched people cry out to God. We watched children get saved with no one leading them to the Lord. It was a glorious time!

We also saw pastors who came into the back of the church to see what would happen. They were amazed as their wives began to dance and shout in the Presence of God. By the end of the night, everybody was dancing and singing. People started to leave after *four hours,* and nobody said one word from the microphone. This happened four nights in a row.

I went there to preach and I couldn't preach. But who wants to hear me when God is in the house? Of course, there are times when we need to teach; but over the past several hundred years, we have made no time for Him to be heard and felt. We have made time for our preaching and our order of worship, but we have made no time for Him.

The Lord is taking His Church back to Himself. Jesus said, "I'll build My own church and the gates of hell won't prevail against it." Pastors just need to be His assistants. We just need to do what He says to do. In fact, Jesus is the One who started it all. He is the One who said, "Whatever I see My Father in Heaven doing, that is what I will do" (see John 5:19). So if I don't see my Father in Heaven doing it, I'm not going to do it.

When Jesus was at the pool of Bethesda, there were hundreds of sick people there. Jesus only saw His Father healing one, so that's the only one He healed. Then He walked away from the pool of Bethesda, leaving hundreds of people still sick (see John 5:1-9). Why did He do that? I have no idea. He is God; and He does what He wants to do. Jesus saw His Father healing only that one person. God will have likewise obedient folks. He is looking for people who will love Him enough to do *only* what He says to do whether somebody else likes it or not. We are not here to please others; we've got to do what God says to do. It can be difficult for ministries today to only pray for one with everyone else sick. But this is our pattern from our Lord. Do only what we see our Father doing, nothing more, nothing less.

Some ridicule the Roman Catholics because they keep God in a box in the front of the church. Well, I contend that we Charismatics are just a little craftier than they are. Our box is in our minds, and we know better than to put it where everybody can see it. We keep our God box where no one can see it. You must be very, very concerned about anybody who says, "God didn't, can't, won't, hasn't, etc.," anything that limits God. He is an ever-expanding God—not constrained by space or time—except when His children restrict His creativity by not believing.

Spiritual Push-Back

There will be men and women who will stand in the gap, saying, "Wait, we will not let you limit God anymore. We have seen Him and we have heard Him." The apostle John said, "That which we have seen and heard and handled of the good Word, this is what we declare to you" (see 1 John 1:3).

We have this same passion as John did! I don't declare theory. I don't declare theology. I'm talking to you about what I have experienced. I'm talking to you about what I have personally experienced and touched of God. I no longer shrink back in silence because someone tries to tell me I am wrong, or ridicules me for my faith. I know who I believe. I know what He has done for me and through me. The evidence I have is my life. I am a changed man. I have seen many miracles and continue to see many miracles in my life and in the lives I am responsible for.

This is called spiritual push-back. Instead of simply falling silent at the accusations of those who do not believe, I will stand my ground. I no longer argue with the blind who try to tell me what a rainbow looks like. In the love and compassion of our Lord, I will now freely declare and even argue with those to whom I am led to be a witness. I will lift my voice without fear.

But there need to be men and women worldwide who will rise up and once and for all push back those who are resisting the Lord and attempting to discredit the work of the cross. Right now, there are many who are ready to rise up and resist the anti-Holy Spirit activity and dark conversation of carnal people.

There have been reports about how the Holy Spirit is moving anew and afresh in places all around the world. We also hear about the opposition to these moves of God. It is important that we understand the difference between what God wants to do and what man wants to do. God will do what He wants to do without our permission. He does not need to ask our opinion. He only asks for our cooperation. Discerning gatekeepers of the Church Jesus is building determine what gets into their church and what gets into the city. If the pastors see something they do not like, it does not get in. But if the pastor sees something that is of the Lord, then the blessing of God falls. When something unusual happens, it is important that the people have a discerning spirit to know what is from the Lord. The church that will change the world is the church that hears from the Lord. We must have a spirit that can touch the Spirit of God. We must have a spirit that can discern what is happening in the spiritual realm, so that as God moves, we can agree and say, "Yes, this is something that God is doing."

If a pastor cannot discern the move of God, or if he is fearful of God out of his control, he will simply close the spiritual gate to the city, as much as it is in his sphere of influence to do so. It is imperative that God's people begin to hear, proclaim, and encourage the genuine work of the Lord among humankind.

The months and the years ahead are going to be extremely challenging. We are going to need God's Presence and power more than we have ever needed it before. The level of power we have had in the past will not withstand the onslaught the enemy will bring us. But God's power is not the problem; He will send as much power as we need to overcome the enemy. The problem is never God's power; the problem is our ability to let God show Himself in new ways. The problem is whether we have the ability to say *yes* to the Lord even when it goes against the traditions we have experienced, the things we believe, or the effects this divine activity might have on our lives personally.

We spend too much of our time being controlled by carnal, angry people who have never experienced the Presence of God. They come speaking in apparent authority, and many are fooled by their words. Many believers are tossed in the waves of an angry sea. They do not know where they are going. They do not know where they came from, and they do not know what is stirring the sea. Knowing the Lord and having spiritual sensitivity will give you strength and assurance to *not* allow yourself to be persuaded only by the words of others, but rather to be persuaded by the spirit of discernment in their hearts. This is the beginning of spiritual push-back.

I have urgency in my spirit that may cause me to say some alarming things. I write them to you out of love and compassion for His children. God wants our hearts open and ready so that whenever He does what He is about to do, there will be people prepared and ready to say *yes* to Him, releasing Him from our control and allowing Him to do things on our behalf that are not a part of the box of tradition, religion, pain, and past. Ultimately, our goal is to allow the Holy Spirit to destroy this box completely. Of course it is a process, but it is a process that, if allowed to continue, will certainly lead you into the glorious liberty of His children.

While confused men and women argue among themselves in the corner, the Kingdom of the living God will rise up and do the will of God.

I am not interested in arguments anymore. Jesus said, "You will know My disciples by their fruit" (see John 15:8). Matthew says that every good tree bears good fruit, but bad trees bear bad fruit (see Matt. 12:33). A good tree can't produce bad fruit any more than a bad tree can produce good fruit. In other words, Jesus is saying, "Don't look at what they say; look at what they are producing." Anybody can sit in the seat of the scornful, and criticize and rebuke and find fault. But it takes men and women of courage, who will not listen to those voices, but who will give themselves to the Spirit of the Lord and examine the fruit, to determine the will of God and determine His activity.

In the Name of Jesus

Living with God out of control and out of the box means recognizing and experiencing the new and exciting activity of God on this planet. You will begin to see healing through the Holy Spirit and redemptive revelation in Christ Jesus. Living with God out of control and out of the box means that we no longer live in a self-made box placed in a self-contained sealed room where we keep God under our control. In fact, the Bible says that we are looking for a city made without hands whose builder and maker is God (see Heb. 11:10). We need to be willing to see things that have not been seen before. Let's not be satisfied with things as they have always been. We must look for the city made without hands, one we have not seen before. We must look for the love of God in ways we have never experienced.

Everything begins to change as soon as I open to hear His voice. For instance, any time I pray a prayer in the name of Jesus, is there anyone else who can answer that prayer? When you pray in the name of Jesus, who answers the prayer? Can the devil answer the prayer prayed in Jesus's name? No! So if my brother is sick and I lay my hand upon him and pray in the name of Jesus, and he is healed, could the devil have healed him?

If I cannot trust the name of Jesus, we are all in big trouble. I cannot then trust Him for anything. When I pray in Jesus's name, I am praying in the power and the authority of the Son of God. Can the enemy push Jesus aside and answer that prayer? What a ridiculous question!

So, to the question, "Who heals in Jesus's name?" Only Jesus, my friend, only Jesus.

Now, this little example probably helped you in clarifying some questions concerning His authority. Your box just got messed with! God is a tad more out of your control than He was a few moments ago. The Lord can and will do this kind of revelation for you as often as you are open.

When we live with God out of our mental box, we will discover a whole new world of God's amazing activity on the earth.

OUT OF THE BOX—INTO CHRIST

Paul demonstrated God's life in power, not just in words—we must do the same. Listen to the apostle Paul:

> *And my message and my preaching were not in persuasive words of wisdom, but in demonstration of the Spirit and of power, so that your faith would not rest on the wisdom of men, but on the power of God. Yet we do speak wisdom among those who are mature; a wisdom, however, not of this age nor of the rulers of this age, who are passing away; but we speak God's wisdom in a mystery, the hidden wisdom which God predestined before the ages to our glory; the wisdom which none of the rulers of this age has understood; for if they had understood it they would not have crucified the Lord of glory; but just as it is written, "Things which eye has not seen and ear has not heard, and which have not entered the heart of man, all that God has prepared for those who love Him" (1 Corinthians 2:4-9).*

Verse 9 is worth another read: *"Things which eye has not seen and ear has not heard, and which have not entered the heart of man, all that God has prepared for those who love Him."* If there are things we have not seen, if there are things we have not heard, if there are things that have never entered into our hearts before, then *there are new things*. There are things we have never experienced. If we are going to go on in the things God wants to do, we have to trust Him that there are things we have not experienced before that we will begin to experience.

If we always do what we have always done, we will always get what we always have had. I don't know about you, but I am not satisfied with what I have always had. Are you satisfied that there are only fifty to one hundred people in most churches? Are you satisfied that there are so few people being healed? I am not satisfied, but we continue to do the same things we have always done.

God is showing us His way, which is really not a new way: It is through His eternal Word. We just haven't seen it before. The Bible is the Word of God, and believers don't want to do anything to violate His Word. But, as mentioned previously, *He* will violate what we think His Word says. He will always challenge our doctrines, He will always challenge our traditions, He will always challenge the way we have always done things, because He has no respect for our old traditions or for a religion that denies the power of God.

Believers are so fearful of heresy that they do not want to risk hearing anything different than what they have always heard. But those who are tired of things as usual will certainly change the world.

SO WHO CHANGES THE WORLD, REALLY?

It is not the intellect that changes the world. If intelligence could change the world, we would have a perfect world. There are many very intelligent people in every country worldwide, but intelligence does not change the world for His glory.

Discernment is simple—it is grown in you during the time you spend in His Presence. The more time you spend in God's Presence, the more discernment you have, because you learn how His Presence feels. You learn how His Presence moves and how He thinks.

Please understand that the world and the religious system wants you to believe your five senses more than it wants you to believe the Holy Spirit. It wants you to trust reason more than it wants you to trust His Presence.

> **Prayer:** *Heavenly Father, we commit ourselves to worshiping You. Whether we are worshiping in church, or whether we are in our car or at home or at work, wherever we can put worship music on, we will put it on and worship the Lord. We commit to continually inviting Your Presence into our lives and continually saying yes to the work of the Holy Spirit. Lord, we have said yes to the devil long enough, and to our own flesh long enough. Please help us to say yes to Jesus, to You, and to the Holy Spirit each and every time You present Yourself to us. In Jesus's name, amen.*

STEWARDING REVIVAL FOR INCREASE

How we respond to the Holy Spirit's movement determines how much of His activity we will experience. In this present season of rain and outpouring, I see the Spirit of God brooding over certain individuals, communities, churches and regions. In many places, however, He is not breaking in with the full force of His power, even though He certainly could do it if He wanted to. So, "why not?"

Increase comes through hungry people—not necessarily people who are going in "kicking and screaming." While God could indeed break out in a sovereign way among people who don't really desire His "disruptive" revival activity, His preference is to subtly move upon a community first, calling forth the hungry. Their hunger then becomes contagious, calling others to pursue the Reviver. It's in these seasons that the Lord gently warms hearts to be prepared to welcome the fullness of His Spirit. I see this happening across the earth right now.

People's hunger for God to move is surpassing their religious backgrounds, denominational prejudices and even their church customs. Because of the urgent hour in which we live, more and more are coming to the realization that we are not living in a time where it is acceptable to play games with religion. While darkness is moving across the earth in pronounced ways, the Bride of Christ is beginning to recognize her divine designation to arise and be the house of His glory. The very Presence of God that proceeds from the throne of God also dwells within us. Where we go, He goes. This is our charge. If we want to see revival increase, it's time for the people of God to carry God into places that need the rains of outpouring. After all, the rain of revival is not going to come down from Heaven; it's going to come out of His anointed vessels—you and I!

In Tommy Tenney's book, *Open Heaven*, he discusses what it means to expand the "throne zone." God is looking for men and women, young and old, who are willing to actually be carriers of His Presence into their everyday lives. No occupation is beyond His reach and no sphere of influence is off-limits.

Read this chapter and allow it to stir up your hunger for a radical expansion of God's Presence. If the wicked city of Nineveh could be turned around—and that was under the Old Testament—what is possible for our city today? Your workplace? Your school? Your university? Your church? If there are carriers of God's Presence occupying these different spheres of society, then there is opportunity for "throne zone" expansion.

CHAPTER 12

EXPANDING THE THRONE ZONE

Tommy Tenney

*I am in pursuit of the "Reviver"—when He
comes to town, revival will come with Him!*

ON EARTH AS IT IS IN HEAVEN

Pastors around the country used to call me to "preach a revival"
in their local churches, hoping I could help them raise excitement levels and perhaps win a few people to the Lord. All that ended the day
my preaching career was ruined by a "hit and run," Jacob-at-Jabbok
encounter with God.

The once respected evangelist they knew has been changed into a
broken, weeping God chaser with a permanent limp and a perpetual
hunger for more. I still burn to see the lost come to Jesus, but I am
no longer interested in the kind of revival where people come to hear

a man preach. I am in pursuit of the "Reviver"—when He comes to town, revival will come with Him!

God changed my "name" in an encounter that dislocated my denominational credentials and withered my dependence on my preaching gift so completely that, much of the time, all I can do is stand before a congregation and weep for His Presence. It is hard to define what I am nowadays, so I basically coined the term, "God chaser," to describe it. But I can tell you what I'm after: I am after a burning bush experience that triggers the release from slavery for everyone within the boundaries of His "throne zone."

A friend of mine coined the term, "throne zone," to describe the atmosphere of worship that goes on around the throne of God. If somehow we can recreate the throne zone on earth as it is in Heaven in our churches and meetings, if our worship becomes so compelling that the manifest Presence of God begins to put itself on display in our midst, then we will see the glory of God begin to flow through our cities. When this happens, the lost will come to Christ on a massive scale that we have never seen before. He said, "If I be lifted up, I will draw all men near" (see John 12:32). We've concentrated on the "drawing" instead of the "lifting"!

This statement is more than a teaching metaphor or a memorable preacher's phrase. It is a spiritual reality revealed in the prophet Ezekiel's vision thousands of years ago.[1] The prophet saw a river (signifying God's glory) flowing out from under the doors of His heavenly sanctuary and into the world, bringing life wherever it went. The depth of the river was shallowest at the sanctuary door, but it got deeper the further it flowed. Natural rivers are shallow at their headwaters or source, and they flow faster, deeper, and wider as they flow toward the sea. This is a picture of "the God-kind of revival."

WHAT HAPPENS WHEN THE GLORY
OF GOD FALLS ON A CITY?

God is able to "do exceedingly abundantly above all that we ask or think" (Eph. 3:20, NKJV), and He wants to do something so big that it is beyond our ability to conceive of its magnitude or dimensions. He has moved upon men in the past, and He has moved upon our generation in a measure. I'm thankful for the way He has visited places like Toronto, Ontario; Pensacola, Florida; Houston, Texas; Baltimore, Maryland; and London, England. (There are countless other places in South America, Africa, Australia, Europe, and the Far East as well.) Yet I have to tell you that we have not yet seen what happens when the glory of God falls on a city. We know what it looks like when God visits a church, but we've not yet seen what it looks like when He visits a city!

A true revival should affect the city like the flood of glory in Ezekiel's vision affected Jerusalem and the nations. It has to happen in the Church first because we set the standard and the pace for what happens in a city. However, what we see in our meetings should be nothing compared to His manifest power revealed in the streets! Acts 2 again, Lord!

FALSE PREMISES ABOUT REVIVAL AND
ANOINTING PRODUCE MISUNDERSTANDING

Sometimes we have false premises about revival and the people God uses in true revivals. These false premises about revival and the anointing can produce a lot of misunderstanding. Someone asked Duncan Campbell to define revival, and he touched on this in his reply:

> First let me tell you what I mean by revival. An evangelistic campaign or a special meeting is not revival. In a successful evangelistic campaign or crusade, there will be

hundreds, even thousands of people making decisions for Jesus Christ, but the community may remain untouched, and the churches continue much the same as before the outreach.

But in revival God moves in the region. Suddenly the community becomes God conscious, and the Spirit of God grips men and women in such a way that even work is given up as people give themselves to waiting upon God. In the midst of the Lewis Awakening [what we call the Hebrides revival], the parish minister...wrote, "The Spirit of the Lord was resting wonderfully on the different townships of the region. His Presence was in the homes of the people, on the meadow, and the moorland, and the public roads."

This Presence of God is the supreme characteristic of a God-sent revival. Of the hundreds who found Jesus Christ during this time, fully 75 percent were saved before they came near a meeting, or heard a sermon by myself or any other minister in the parish. The power of God was moving in an operation that the fear of God gripped the souls of men before they ever reached the meetings.[2]

I will never be content merely to see the glory of God flow down the beautiful carpeted aisles of our churches. I want to see it flow down Main Street in an uncontrollable, unstoppable flood of glory that carries along everything in its path. I want His glory to invade the malls, grocery stores, health spas, and bars across town. I want to hear unchurched people say that they had to abandon an expensive entrée at their favorite restaurant to follow the dripping trail of God's glory to a church somewhere and demand, "Somebody tell me what to do!"

If good sermons and good songs were going to save the world, it would already be saved. There's a missing ingredient, and that "Divine Ingredient" is knocking at the door. The Hebrides revival provides a brief hint of what happens when glory breaks out. While describing the first days of the movement in the Hebrides Islands, Duncan Campbell remembered closing out a service in a crowded church and noticing that the congregation seemed reluctant to disperse. Many of the people just stood outside of the church building in a silence that was almost tense.

> "Suddenly a cry is heard within, a young man burdened for the souls of his fellow men is pouring out his soul in intercession." Campbell said the man prayed until he collapsed and lay prostrate on the floor of the church building. He said, "The congregation, moved by a power they could not resist, came back into the church, and a wave of conviction swept over the gathering, moving strong men to cry to God for mercy."[3]

"GOD, YOU PROMISED!"

I asked an English friend about this incident, and it turns out he had heard Duncan Campbell speak about it. He told me, "Most of the people had already left the church according to Mr. Campbell, but he said, 'The postman stood up and prayed, and then this young man stood up. I'll never forget the words he said: "Oh God, You promised!" All of a sudden it sounded like chariot wheels were rumbling on the roof of the church building. The next thing we knew, the church was filling back up again!'"

They learned later that many of the people had already started home when they suddenly felt the call to retrace their steps and return to the church building to pray. During some points of the Hebrides revival, Campbell said, "Most of them [the converts to Christ] only came to church to tell us that they had been converted because they would be weaving at a loom, or they would be plowing in the field when God would convict them. They just showed up to say, 'Where do I join, and what do I do?'"[4]

I am so tired of the manipulations of men supplanting the glory of God, thinking that the silly sermons they preach or the songs they sing is what causes anything! He is the root cause. If we don't have a sovereign visitation of God, we are in trouble. We must stop looking to man. Where are the young men (or the old, or the women!) who will stand in our midst, and say, "God, You promised"?

We need to stop looking to the platform for the power of God. We have put enormous pressure on the servants of God to try to manipulate and create what can only come from God. We need to wait on Him and seek Him until something breaks in the heavens!

The Voice of Prayer Mingled with the Groans of the Repentant

According to Duncan Campbell, this divine visitation just continued. They tasted a measure of divine habitation that rocked the region.

> One evening, as the congregation was leaving the church and moving down toward the main road, the Spirit of God fell on the people in a Pentecostal power, no other word can describe it. In a few minutes the awareness of the Presence of the Most High became so wonderful and so subduing, that one could only say with Jacob of old, "Surely the Lord is in this place." And there under the open heavens, and by the roadside, the voice of prayer was mingled with the groans of the repentant as free grace awoke men with light from on high.
>
> Soon the whole island was in the grip of a mighty movement of the Spirit, bringing deep conviction of sin and a hunger for God. This movement was different than the other islands, and that while in Lewis [island] there were physical manifestations and prostrations, there were not here, but the work was as deep, and the result was enduring.[5]

This is a picture, a foretaste, of God's will for the Church today.

It is up to the Church to birth the purposes of God in this generation. During the years I pastored a church, I used to tell couples expecting their first baby, "I need to tell you that when your baby is born, your whole life will change."

Their typical answer was sort of a nod and a smile, "Yeah, yeah, we understand."

I wanted to just take them by the shoulders and look them in the eye and say once more, "No, no, you don't understand! In fact, you don't even have a clue. You think you do, but you really don't."

WE DON'T HAVE A CLUE

Too many of us sit together in our "revival" meetings and nod and smile and say, "Yeah, we know what revival is, and we are ready for it." The truth is that we don't have a clue. The original purpose of the Church was to be a meeting place between God and man, not a glorified "bless me" club or a receiving place where man comes solely to receive from God. Church was not created as a spiritual bless-me trough where we can roll in the anointing and pig out. Church was created for you to give something of yourself to Him.

If we want to restore the Church to its original power, we must return to God's original recipe for revival in Second Chronicles 7:14: "If My people who are called by My name will humble themselves, and pray..." (NKJV). The next phrase reveals the step that goes beyond prayer. God says, "and seek My face." We think we know everything there is to know about prayer. We say we understand prayer, and we recite prayers, we can even prevail in prayer. Yet I wonder how many of us fully understand God's command in Second Chronicles to seek His face? We must seek the face of God, not His hand. Prayer is petitioning—"seeking His face" is positioning.

We must abandon the entertainment-based worship that tickles our ears and encourages our selfish desires to constantly hear something, feel something, or do something that makes us feel good. Aren't you hungry for more? Someday, somewhere, we will meet to seek His face and the glory of God will settle down among us. When that happens, we won't leave that place with just a temporary touch of God's anointing. Everyone who sees His glory will leave dramatically different than before He came.

PICTURE THE GLORY OF GOD RIVETING ENTIRE COMMUNITIES

We need mass Damascus Road experiences, where the glory of God is revealed to an entire assembly of people all at once. In a moment of time, God's manifest Presence transformed Saul of Tarsus from a persecutor into a propagator of the Gospel. Now picture the glory of God riveting entire communities with conviction after engulfing them in the light of His glory!

This is the way to win the lost. If worship is done right, then soulwinning and altar calls don't take a whole lot of words. Simply say, "Come," and they will. Why? Worship brings God's Presence, and His Presence drives away everything else. That means people in the throne zone may be given, for the first time, the opportunity of an unfettered choice when His Presence comes.

The coming revival is not going to be about sermons and information; it's going to be about worship and impartation. The preaching of the Word won't stop, but the sermons that come will serve the same purpose as Peter's impromptu sermon on the Day of Pentecost. They won't necessarily produce desired actions in people; they will come after the fact to explain what happened after "God came down." (Right now, we tend to preach by faith before the fact and hope it will happen.) Worship draws down the Presence of God.

The "Suddenly of God" Requires the "Waiting of Man"

"Suddenly" there came an upper-room experience where He threw open the windows of Heaven and rushed down. That's what we want—the rushing in of God, that suddenly of God. But you don't have the "suddenly of God" without the "waiting of man." We need to go after the face of God. We can no longer be content with God just slipping His hand out from under the veil to dispense Gospel goodies to us anymore. We want the veil to open, and we want to pass through into the Holy of Holies to have a life-changing encounter with Him. Then we need to prop open that veil with Davidic passion and worship so the glory of God will manifest itself in the streets of the city.

The Church is pregnant with God's purposes. Our body feels swollen; our belly is distended. We don't know when or where the baby will be born, but we know a baby is about to be born, and we are desperate. To be honest, I hope you live with so much holy frustration that you can't sleep tonight. I pray that a gnawing hunger for the Presence of God rises up in your heart with devastating results. I want you to be "ruined" for everything except His purposes.

On the day the Church rises up to build a mercy seat according to the pattern of Heaven, God will wave good-bye to Michael and Gabriel and will literally set up a throne zone in our midst! Let me assure you that when the glory of God shows up like that, we won't have to advertise or promote anything. Once the Bread of Heaven takes His seat among us, the hungry will come.

"Father, we fan the flames of hunger.

May we never be the same. Set our hearts on fire."

There is only one way you and I can pay the price of obedience to create a throne zone on earth. We need to let our hearts be so broken before Him that the things that break His heart also break our hearts.

Put your hand on your heart and, if you dare, pray this prayer:

"Break my heart, Lord;

I don't want to be the same.

Soften my heart, Lord Jesus,

and let me dwell in Your Presence."

THE FAIL-SAFE WAY TO OPEN HEAVEN'S GATES

There is one fail-safe way to open the gates of Heaven and close the gates of hell on the ruling principalities and powers of darkness in your region. Pray, repent, intercede, and worship God until you break open a hole in the heavens and God flips on His glory light switch. Satanic forces will flee in every direction!

Even our best "spiritual warfare" and our loudest screams against demonic forces can't compare with the power released when God turns on the light of His glory. The status quo isn't working. We can't get the world into our church buildings—our lifestyles have convinced people that we don't have anything to offer them. We must get the "God of the Church" to them.

It is up to us. We can remain satisfied with our bland diets of powerless services interspersed with a few "good" services each year, or we can pursue God at any cost. Most of us are uncomfortable with change, but change is a part of what God is about to do. He is redefining the Church and making our religious labels totally obsolete. I can tell you this much about it: His manifest Presence is going to be supreme. That means it won't really matter who speaks, who sings, who prays, or who does anything in those services—as long as He is there.

CAUGHT IN AN OUTBREAK OF HIS PRESENCE!

People don't understand what it means to be caught in an outbreak of the manifest Presence of God. Duncan Campbell described an incident in the Hebrides that was burned into his memory.

> At my request several officers from the parish visited the island, bringing with them a young lad who recently was brought to the saving knowledge. After spending time and prayer at the cottage, we went to the church to find it crowded now. But seldom did I experience such bondage of spirit, and preaching was most difficult, so much so that when only half way through my address I stopped preaching.
>
> Just then my eye caught sight of this young lad who was visibly moved, and appeared to be deeply burdened. Leaning over the pulpit I said, "Donald, will you lead us in prayer." There was an immediate response, and in that moment the flood gates of heaven opened, and the congregation was struck as by a hurricane, and many cried out for mercy.
>
> But the most remarkable feature of this visitation was not what happened there in the church, but the spiritual impact on the island. Men, who until that moment had no thought of seeking after God, were suddenly arrested where they stood, sat or laid, and became deeply concerned about their soul, until they said, This is the Lord's doing.[6]

I WANT THE HEAVENS TO BREAK OVER ENTIRE CITIES

I'm sick of reading from the menu of programmed revival. I want the heavens to break open over entire cities, but the Church knows very little about this type of evangelism. Our specialty seems to be "program evangelism." We know how to make phone calls, mail letters, and knock on doors in an organized way to win souls to Christ, and I'm thankful for every soul that has come to Christ through these methods.

We also know about "power evangelism," the method of soul winning introduced to American churches nearly 20 years ago by the late John Wimber. This is also a program, but it mixes the healing anointing with organized evangelism outreach.

We must learn how to attract God to the Church in such a way that He can manifest His glory freely. When that happens, we won't have to worry about attracting men. God will do it Himself. "Presence" evangelism occurs when Jesus is lifted up in all His glory, because He promised that He will draw all men to Himself (see John 12:32). When we take on the responsibility of attracting people to the church, all we get is a crowd.

We try to attract man, thinking that's our job. When are we going to learn? The primary purpose of the Church is to attract Him!

The bottom line is simply this: We need more of God and less of man. We need people who will pray until the heavens collapse, crying out, "God, You promised!"

You may be right at the door to the throne zone this very moment. God wants to meet you where you are. You can leave this divine appointment with an impartation from God that can bring revival to your church and city and bring the prodigals home in your family. But no one can do it for you. You must personally walk through that door of death called repentance. The glory of God is waiting just on the other side, but only dead men can see His face. Only beaten worshipers can build the mercy seat through their broken, purified, and repentant worship. It is just possible that you might be the "somebody" who will change the destiny of a nation.

When people asked John Wesley how he drew such large crowds and led so many people to Christ, he told them, "I just set myself on fire for God and people come to see me burn." Somebody has to start the fire. If not you, then who? If not here and now, then where and when? Just remember that you have no right to pray for the fire of God unless you are willing to be the fuel of God!

I COULDN'T RUN ANYMORE!

Miraculous things happen when God's glory begins to settle down over a place. I know of a church in Georgia where an outbreak of God began to invade the community outside the church building. The testimony of one woman illustrates in a trickle what I'm praying for in a torrent. She told me:

> Three Sundays ago I was sitting in my living room about a half mile away from the church. I didn't know what it was, but a spirit, a Presence of God entered my living room. I was sitting there smoking a Marlboro cigarette, drinking Bud Light, and channel surfing when the Presence of God just came into my living room. I ran from it at first. In fact, I got up and moved into the kitchen.
>
> The first week I could go from the kitchen to the living room. The Presence was only in the living room, not the kitchen. Last week, it not only came in the living room, but it invaded the kitchen, so I went to my bedroom.
>
> This morning when I got up, it had pushed all the way into my bedroom and I couldn't run anymore! I knew it was coming from here, and I just had to come.

That woman was saved that night, and her testimony perfectly illustrates the way "Presence evangelism" invades a city. If you take her testimony and multiply it by hundreds, thousands, and millions of lives, you might have a glimpse of what God has in store for this generation if we can create a throne zone of His Presence that just keeps pushing through the city. When that happens, people won't be able to run anymore because mercy and grace will be flowing through the streets of the city. This river of glory will only get wider and deeper the further it goes. God, do it!

> *Father, impart to us a broken heart, as Your heart was broken, and let beaten winged worshipers build a place of habitation. We turn our back on what is good to seek what is best. We want Your kabod, Your glory, O God. Father, thank You for the anointing and for what it does. But it still smells like man. We pray, "Let man die, and let the glory of God come."*

Somebody needs to pray the prayer of Moses, "Show me Your glory!" We need the glory of God in our churches, homes, and public schools. I look for the day some young person will bow his or her head to pray in the public school lunchroom and the glory of God suddenly fall on the entire school! We've had the blood of students flow in the hallways—it's time for the blood of Jesus to flow in the schools!

HE WILL ONLY COME THROUGH THE CRACKS OF OUR BROKENNESS

We need God in our midst. If we build the mercy seat, He will come. If we want God to show up in our churches, He will only come through the cracks of our brokenness, not through the wholeness of our arrogance. Only broken earthly vessels can hold the heavenly glory. It doesn't make sense, but it is true.

I can't pray anything upon you except my hunger. I am hungry for God, and He promised us that He would meet that need: "Blessed are those who hunger and thirst...for they shall be filled" (Matt. 5:6, NKJV). The glory cannot come to a full vessel. We must cry out for more of Him and less of us. We must empty our cups of "self" before He can fill them up with Himself. It is the only way to open the heavens and release the glory of God over our cities.

Can you imagine what will happen if we empty ourselves and His manifest Presence comes? What will happen when God's manifest Presence settles over a church in a city? We must create a throne zone and expand the parameters of the manifest Presence of God where His glory is made available to everyone without a veil, a wall, or a gate.

When there is no barrier between God and man, you will hear Him if He whispers. It won't take a hurricane-force wind of God to move you; rather it will be just the gentlest zephyr, the smallest breeze, the lightest whisper from His heart. If we can create such a place through our repentant "beaten" worship, God will come. David's tabernacle was His "favorite house" because of its unveiled worship of intimacy. It is this atmosphere of intimacy that creates a place of divine habitation—a "throne zone" on earth as in Heaven—God's favorite house.

Jesus, let Your glory flow, let it flow. We seek Your face.

ENDNOTES

1. I also discussed this timely passage from Ezekiel 47 in *The God Chasers* (Shippensburg, PA: Destiny Image Publishers, 1998), 106-107.

2. Duncan Campbell, from conversations with Alan Vincent. These remarks by Duncan Campbell are available on audiotapes from the GodChasers.network at P.O. Box 3355, Pineville, Louisiana 71361, or from the website, www.GodChasers.net.

3. Ibid.

4. Ibid.

5. Ibid.

6. Ibid.

The end goal of revival? Create a further dissatisfaction within us that drives us to cry out for "more." It's as if we are finishing right where we started—holy discontentment. Revival, in some ways, is cyclical. We're discontent with status quo Christianity. We press in and cry out for a "move of God." We experience the move of God. We steward it. We celebrate it. We receive the rain. But then what? We are called to be expansion agents of outpouring. The key to seeing more is staying hungry.

How do we stay hungry? While there are many practical ways to maintain our desire for the Spirit's movement, Jesus gave us the greatest safeguard against stagnancy when He made the following promise:

> *"Truly, truly, I say to you, whoever believes in me will also do the works that I do; and greater works than these will he do, because I am going to the Father"* (John 14:12).

Are we walking in the greater works yet? As long as there is opportunity for greater works to be performed, then we are still charged with the sacred responsibility of crying out for more.

God is positioning His people for a glorious end-time revival. How long will this move of God continue? Until the day Jesus visibly returns to planet earth. Until then, outpouring will only increase. Heaven has it sights sets on "all flesh," as such was the objective of outpouring beginning on the Day of Pentecost.

Once holy discontentment births revival prayer, and revival prayer produces a people who carry God's glory, expanding that zone of His manifest Presence, we will see the works of revival demonstrated. We are seeing these in part, right now. We are seeing sinners transformed by the saving grace of Jesus Christ. We are seeing broken lives supernaturally healed and mended. We are seeing relationships miraculously restored, bodies healed, torment broken, depression dispelled, and other evidences of an in-breaking Kingdom. We celebrate this all. In fact, Scripture is filled with invitations for us to remember the works of God. And yet, how we remember determines whether we ask for more.

Bill Johnson's *When Heaven Invades Earth* is a contemporary treatise on what the normal Christian life looks like in full Biblical operation. It is fundamentally supernatural. Miracles, signs and wonders should be normative, not the exception. The body of Christ is awakening to this reality in an unusual way. At the same time, Bill provides a wonderful perspective on moving forward, navigating the ever-rising waters of outpouring. Even though what we are experiencing in this hour is, for all intents and purposes, an expression of revival, there is more to see, there is more to discover, there is more to experience, and there is more to release.

The revival rain that is presently falling cannot become a memory that future generations speak of nostalgically and move on. Heaven forbid. It is our responsibility to steward the moment we have been given. Right here, right now. The rain is falling. What will protect this present revival from one day becoming a relic of history is how we respond to what God is currently doing. Some become satisfied with the present measure of rain. We celebrate it, yes. We offer thanksgiving for sure. But we recognize that since the Kingdom is ever increasing and the reign of God is expanding, we have a Great Commission to see all nations, all flesh, and all creation come into collision with this great outpouring.

CHAPTER 13

THIS PRESENT REVIVAL

Bill Johnson

*What God has planned for the Church in this hour
is greater than our ability to imagine and pray.
We must have the help of the Holy Spirit to learn
about these mysteries of the Church and God's
Kingdom. Without Him we don't have enough
insight even to know what to ask for in prayer.*

Understanding what is about to come is important, but not to equip us to plan and strategize more effectively. On the contrary, it's important to understand God's promise and purpose for the Church so that we might become dissatisfied—so that we will become desperate. Intercession from insatiable hunger moves the heart of God as nothing else can.

Revival is not for the faint of heart. It brings fear to the complacent because of the risks it requires. The fearful often work against the move of God—sometimes to their death—all the while thinking they are working for Him. Deception says that the changes brought about by revival contradict the faith of their fathers. As a result, the God-given ability to create withers into the laborious task of preserving. The fearful become curators of museums instead of builders of the Kingdom.

Others are ready to risk all. The faith of their fathers is considered a worthy foundation to build upon. They have caught a glimpse of what could be and will settle for nothing less. Change is not a threat, but an adventure. Revelation increases, ideas multiply, and the stretch begins.

"The Lord God does nothing unless He reveals His secret counsel to His servants the prophets" (Amos 3:7, NASB). God's activities on earth begin with a revelation to mankind. The prophet hears and declares. Those with ears to hear respond and are equipped for change.

In order to understand who we are and what we are to become, we must see Jesus *as He is*. We are about to see the difference between the Jesus who walked the streets healing the sick and raising the dead, and the Jesus who today reigns over all. As glorious as His life was on earth, it was the *before* side of the cross. Christianity is life on the resurrection side of the cross.

This shift in focus will come in these last days. It must happen if we are to become what He has purposed for us.

Religion (which is "form without power") will be more and more despised in the hearts of those who truly belong to Him. Revelation creates an appetite for Him. He doesn't come in a "no frills" model. There's no economy-class Holy Spirit. He only comes fully equipped. He is loaded, full of power and glory. And He wants to be seen as He is, in us.

A GREATER CONCEPT

The power of one word from His mouth can create a galaxy. His promises for the Church are beyond all comprehension. Too many consider them to be God's promise either for the Millennium or Heaven, claiming that to emphasize God's plan for now instead of eternity is to dishonor the fact that Jesus has gone to prepare a place for us. Our predisposition toward a weak Church has blinded our eyes to the truths of God's Word about us. This problem is rooted in our unbelief, not in our hunger for Heaven. Jesus taught us how to live by announcing, "The Kingdom of God is at hand!" It is a present reality, affecting the *now*.

We lack understanding of who we are because we have little revelation of who He is. We know a lot about His life on earth. The Gospels are filled with information about what He was like, how He lived, and what He did. Yet that is not the example of what the Church is to become. What He is today, glorified, seated at the right hand of the Father, is the model for what we are becoming!

Consider the opening statement: *What God has planned for the Church in this hour is greater than our ability to imagine and pray.* Such statements cause some to fear the Church will not be balanced. Many say that we must be careful over how much emphasis we put on what we are to become *in the now*. Why? For the most part it is a fear of disappointment that creates such caution. Fear of disappointment has justified our unbelief. What is the worst that could happen if I pursued what is reserved for eternity? God could say, *No!* We make a big mistake to think we can figure out what has been reserved for Heaven, from this side of Heaven.

Because many fear excess, mediocrity is embraced as balance. Such fear makes complacency a virtue. And it's the fear of excess that has made those that are resistant to change appear noble minded. Excess has never brought an end to revival. William DeArteaga states, "The Great Awakening was not quenched because of its extremists. It was quenched because of the condemnation of its opponents."[1] He also says, "Divisions occur whenever the intellect is enthroned as the measure of spirituality—not because spiritual gifts are exercised, as many charge."[2] I pay no attention to the warnings of possible excess from those who are satisfied with lack.

This generation is a generation of risk takers. And not all the risks taken will be seen as real faith. Some will come to light as steps of foolishness and presumption. But they must be taken just the same. How else can we learn? Make room for risk takers in your life that don't *bat a thousand*. They will inspire you to the greatness available in serving a great God.

The local steelhead fishermen say, "If you don't get your rig snagged on the bottom of the river now and then, you're not fishing deep enough." While I don't want to honor presumption or error, I do want to applaud passion and effort. Our obsession with perfection has given place to some of our greatest blemishes. When I taught my sons to ride a bike I took them to the park where there was lots of grass. Why? Because I wanted them not to get hurt *when* they fell. It was not a question of *if*. The addiction to perfection has given place to a religious spirit. People who refuse to step out and be used by God become the critics of those who do. Risk takers, the ones who thrill the heart of God, become the targets of those who never fail because they seldom try.

THE COMING GLORIOUS CHURCH...

The following is a *partial* list of things that are mentioned in Scripture about the Church that have yet to be fulfilled. Jesus intends for us to become mature before He returns. Each of these passages provides a prophetic glimpse into the heart of God for us right now.

Wisdom of God

> *That now the manifold **wisdom** of God might be made known by the church to the principalities and powers in the heavenly places, according to His eternal purpose...* (Ephesians 3:10-11, NKJV).

Wisdom is to be displayed by us NOW! It is clear that God intends to teach the spirit realm about His wisdom through those made in His image—us.

Solomon was the wisest man ever to live, apart from Jesus who is wisdom personified (see 1 Cor. 1:30). The queen of Sheba came to examine Solomon's wisdom. "And when the queen of Sheba had seen the wisdom of Solomon, the house that he had built, the food on his table, the seating of his servants, the service of his waiters and their apparel, his cupbearers and their apparel, and his entryway by which he went up to the house of the Lord, there was no more spirit in her" (2 Chron. 9:4, NKJV). She acknowledged that his wisdom was far greater than she ever imagined. The depth of his wisdom was actually identified by these three attributes: *excellence, creativity,* and *integrity.* When she saw it in action, it took her breath away!

The wisdom of God will again be seen in His people. The Church, which is presently despised, or at best ignored, will again be reverenced and admired. The Church will again be a praise in the earth (see Jer. 33:9).

Let's examine the three elements belonging to Solomon's wisdom:

Excellence is the high standard for what we do because of who we are. God is extravagant, but not wasteful. An excellent heart for God may appear to be wasteful to those on the outside. For example: In Matthew 26:8-9 we find Mary pouring out an ointment upon Jesus that cost a full year's income. The disciples thought it would be put to better use if it would have been sold and the money given to the poor. In Second Samuel 6:14-16,23, King David humbled himself before the people by taking off his kingly garments and dancing wildly before God. His wife, Michal, despised him for it. As a result she bore no children to the day of her death—either from barrenness or from the lack of intimacy between her and her husband, David. It was a tragic loss caused by pride. In both situations outsiders considered the extravagant actions of these worshipers to be wasteful. God is good. Excellence comes from viewing things from His perspective.

In pursuing this virtue, we do all to the glory of God, with all our might. A heart of excellence has no place for the poverty spirit that affects so much of what we do.

Creativity is not only seen in a full restoration of the arts, but is the nature of His people in finding new and better ways to do things. It is a shame for the Church to fall into the rut of predictability and call it tradition. We must reveal who our Father is through creative expression.

The Church is often guilty of avoiding creativity because it requires change. Resistance to change is a resistance to the nature of God. Because the winds of change are blowing, it will be easy to distinguish between those who are satisfied and those who are hungry. Change brings to light the secrets of the heart.

This anointing will also bring about new inventions, breakthroughs in medicine and science, and novel ideas for business and education. New sounds of music will come from the Church, as will other forms of art. The list is endless. The sky is the limit. Arise and create!

Integrity is the expression of God's character seen in us. And that character is His holiness. Holiness is the essence of His nature. It is not something He does or doesn't do. It is who He is. It is the same for us. We are holy because the nature of God is in us. It begins with a heart separated unto God, and becomes evident in the Christ nature seen through us.

If we can keep the soiled hands of religion from the beautiful expression of God holiness, people will be attracted to the Church as they were to Jesus. Religion is not only boring; it is cruel. It takes the breath out of every good thing. True holiness is refreshingly good.

The queen of Sheba became speechless in response to Solomon's wisdom. It's time for the Church's wisdom to cause the world to become silent again.

Glorious Church

> ...that He might present her to Himself a **glorious church** (Ephesians 5:27, NKJV).

God's original intent for mankind is seen in the passage, "For all have sinned and fall short of the glory of God" (Rom. 3:23). We were to live in the glory of God. That was the target when God created mankind. Our sin caused the arrow of His purpose to fall short.

The glory of God is the manifested Presence of Jesus. Imagine this: A people that are continually conscious of the Presence of God, not in theory, but the actual Presence of God upon them!

We will be a Church in which Jesus is seen in His glory! It is the Holy Spirit's Presence and anointing that will dominate the Christian's life. The Church will be radiant. "The latter glory of this house will be greater than the former" (Hag. 2:9, NASB).

Bride Without Spot or Wrinkle

> ...that He might present her to Himself a glorious church, **not having spot or wrinkle** or any such thing, but that she should be holy and without blemish (Ephesians 5:27, NKJV).

Imagine a beautiful young woman prepared for a wedding. She has taken care of herself by eating right and getting all the exercise she needs. Her mind is sharp and she is emotionally secure and free. By looking at her, you'd never know she had ever done anything wrong. Guilt and shame do not blemish her countenance. She understands and exudes grace. According to Revelation 19:7, she made herself ready. Romance will do that to you. As Larry Randolph puts it, "It's a perversion to expect the groom to dress the bride for the wedding." The Church is to make herself ready. The tools are in place for such an event. The Church must now use them.

The former is a biblical description of the Bride of Christ. When we see how great God is, we'll not question His ability to pull this one off. Paul makes a statement to the church at Corinth that he didn't want to return to them until their obedience was complete. That is the heart of God for the Church. And so, Jesus, *the perfect One*, will return for *the spotless one* when He views our obedience as complete.

Unity of Faith

> *...till we all come to the* **unity of the faith**... (Ephesians 4:13, NKJV).

This that is called the *unity of faith* is the *faith that works through love* mentioned in Galatians 5:6. Love and faith are the two essentials of the Christian life.

Faith comes from the Word of God, specifically *"a word freshly spoken."* Faith is what pleases God. It is active trust in Him as Abba Father. He alone is the source of such faith. It comes as the result of Him speaking to His people. Unity of faith means we will hear His voice together, and demonstrate great exploits. It is a lifestyle, not just a concept—as in having *unity in our ideas about faith*. The exploits of the present and coming revival will surpass all the accomplishments of the Church in all history combined. Over 1 billion souls will be saved. Stadiums will be filled with people 24 hours a day, for days on end, with miracles beyond number: healings, conversions, resurrections, and deliverances too many to count. No special speaker, no well-known miracle worker, just the Church being what God has called her to be. And all this will be the outgrowth of the *unity of faith*.

Revelation Knowledge of the Son

> *...till we all come to the unity of the faith and of the* **knowledge of the Son of God**... (Ephesians 4:13, NKJV).

The apostle John once laid his head on the chest of Jesus. He was called the one whom Jesus loved. Toward the end of his life, on the Isles of Patmos, he saw Jesus again. This time Jesus looked nothing like the one he shared that final meal with. His hair was white like wool, His eyes were a flame of fire, and His feet were like burnished bronze. God felt that this revelation was worthy of a book. It is called: The Revelation of Jesus Christ. The entire Church will receive a fresh revelation of Jesus Christ, especially through that book. This that has been so mysterious will be understood. And that revelation will launch the Church into a transformation unlike any experienced in a previous age. Why? *Because as we see Him, we become like Him!*

If the revelation of Jesus is the primary focus of the book of Revelation, then we'd also have to admit that worship is the central response. The coming increase in revelation of Jesus will be measurable through new dimensions of worship—corporate throne room experiences.

A Mature Man

> *...till we all come to the unity of the faith and of the* *knowledge of the Son of God, to* **a perfect man**... (Ephesians 4:13, NKJV).

An Olympic athlete will never get to the games by gifting alone. It's the powerful combination of a gift brought to its full potential through discipline. That is the picture of the Church becoming a mature man. It is singular, meaning we all function together as one. All its members will work in perfect coordination and harmony, complementing each other's function and gift, according to the directions given by the head. This was not a promise to be fulfilled in eternity.

While I don't believe that this is speaking of human perfection, I do believe there is a maturity of function, without jealousy, that will develop as His Presence becomes more manifest. We need to embrace this as possible because He said it is.

Filled With the Fullness of God

> ...to know the love of Christ which passes knowledge; that you may be **filled with all the fullness of God** (Ephesians 3:19, NKJV).

Imagine a house with many rooms. This house represents our life. Every room that we allow His love to touch becomes filled with His fullness. That is the picture of this verse. The Church will know the love of God by experience. This will go beyond our ability to comprehend. That intimate love relationship with God will help us to receive all that He has desired to release since the beginning of time.

> ...till we all come to the unity of the faith and of the knowledge of the Son of God, to a perfect man, to the measure of the stature of the fullness of Christ (Ephesians 4:13, NKJV).

The experiential love of God, and the corresponding fullness of the Spirit is what is necessary to bring us to the full *stature of Christ—Jesus will be accurately seen in the Church, just as the Father was accurately seen in Jesus.*

Gifts of the Spirit Fully Expressed

> And it shall come to pass in the last days, says God, that I will pour out of My Spirit on **all flesh**; your **sons** and your **daughters** shall prophesy, your **young** men shall see visions, your **old** men shall dream dreams. And on My **menservants** and on My **maidservants**

> *I will pour out My Spirit in those days; and **they** shall prophesy* (Acts 2:17-18, NKJV).

This passage quoted from Joel 2 has never been completely fulfilled. It had initial fulfillment in Acts 2, but its reach was far greater than that generation could fulfill. First of all, *All flesh* was never touched by that revival. But it will happen. In the coming move of God, racial barriers will be broken, as will the economic, sexual, and age barriers. The outpouring of the Spirit in the last generation will touch every nation on the earth, releasing the gifts of the Spirit in full measure upon and through His people.

First Corinthians 12–14 is a wonderful teaching on the operation of the gifts of the Spirit. But it is so much more. It is a revelation of a body of believers who live in the realm of the Spirit that is essential for last days' ministry. These manifestations of the Holy Spirit will be taken to the streets where they belong. It is there that they reach their full potential.

This generation will fulfill the cry of Moses for all of God's people to be prophets. We will carry the Elijah anointing in preparing for the return of the Lord in the same way that John the Baptist carried the Elijah anointing and prepared the people for the coming of the Lord.

Greater Works

> *...He who believes in Me, the works that I do he will do also; and **greater works** than these he will do, because I go to My Father* (John 14:12, NKJV).

Jesus's prophecy of us doing greater works than He did has stirred the Church to look for some abstract meaning to this very simple statement. Many theologians seek to honor the works of Jesus as unattainable, which is religion fathered by unbelief. It does not impress God to ignore what He promised under the guise of honoring the work of Jesus on the earth. Jesus's statement is not that hard to understand. *Greater* means "greater." And the *works* He referred to are signs and wonders. It will not be a disservice to Him to have a generation obey Him, and go beyond His own *high-water mark*. He showed us what one person could do who has the Spirit without measure. What could millions do? That was His point, and it became His prophecy.

This verse is often explained away by saying it refers to *quantity* of works, not *quality*. As you can see, millions of people should be able to surpass the sheer number of works that Jesus did simply because we are so many. But that waters down the intent of His statement. The word greater is *mizon* in the Greek. It is found 45 times in the New Testament. It is always used to describe "quality," not quantity.

Thy Kingdom Come

> *Your kingdom come. Your will be done on earth as it is in heaven* (Matthew 6:10).

He's not the kind of Father who gives us a command to ask for something without fully intending to answer our request. He directs us to pray this prayer because it is in His heart to fulfill it. The safest prayers in existence are the ones He tells us to pray. His answer will be *beyond all we could ask or think*. And it is *"according to the power that works in us"* (Eph. 3:20, NKJV).

Jesus said that He would be returning after the Gospel of the Kingdom is preached in all the world—then the end would come (see Matt. 24:14). The present day understanding of *preaching the gospel of the Kingdom* means to preach a message that will bring as many people to conversion as possible. But what did preaching the Gospel of the Kingdom mean to Jesus? Every instance in which He either did it, or commanded it, miracles followed. The message was to be a declaration of His lordship and dominion over all things, followed by demonstrations of power, illustrating that His world is invading ours through signs and wonders. Consider what is meant by this promise: There will be a generation of *believers* that will preach as He did, doing what He did, in every nation of the world before the end comes! That is quite a promise.

The present reality of the Kingdom will become manifest and realized in the everyday life of the believer. That world will break into this one at every point where the Christian prays in faith. The lordship of Jesus will be seen, and the bounty of His rule will be experienced. While the full expression of His Kingdom may be reserved for eternity, it has never entered our minds what God would like to do before then. It's time to explore that possibility.

THE EXPLOSIVE CHURCH

Wouldn't it be wonderful to have churches so explosive in the supernatural that we would have to find ways to calm them down? That's what Paul had to do with the Corinthian church. The instructions about the gifts of the Spirit were given to a people who had so much they needed to organize it. "All things should be done decently and in order" (1 Cor. 14:40). You can't organize what you don't have. *Everything* has to be done before you can add a structure to make it more effective. Order is a poor substitute for power. But if you have much power, you'll need good order. *Only in that case* will order add a new dimension to the role of power in the Church.

LOVING PEOPLE, NOT THEIR IDEAS

In discussing the present move of God with a cessationist,[3] he told me that I was under deception because of my pursuit of a gospel of power. He informed me that all miracles ended with the death of the last of the twelve apostles. He further stated that the miracles of healing, the testimonies of restored families, the new zeal for the Scriptures, and the passion to give a witness of God's love to others was probably a work of the devil. I told him that his devil was too big and his God was too small. In order to feel good about our present condition, the Church has created doctrines to justify weaknesses.

195

Some have even made those deficiencies seem like strengths. These are doctrines of demons! While I love and honor people who believe such things, I feel no need to honor such nonsense.

We are the most to be pitied if we think we've reached the fullness of what God intended for His Church here on earth. All Church history is built on partial revelation. Everything that has happened in the Church over the past 1,900 years has fallen short of what the early Church had and lost. Each move of God has been followed by another, just to restore what was forfeited and forgotten. And we still haven't arrived to the standard that they attained, let alone surpassed it. Yet, not even the early Church fulfilled God's full intention for His people. That privilege was reserved for those in the last leg of the race. It is our destiny.

As wonderful as our spiritual roots are, they are insufficient. What was good for *yesterday* is deficient for *today*. To insist that we stay with what our fathers fought for is to insult our forefathers. They risked all to pursue something fresh and new in God. It's not that *everything* must change for us to flow with what God is saying and doing. It's just that we make too many assumptions about the *rightness* of what presently exists. Those assumptions blind us to the revelations still contained in Scripture. In reality, what we think of as the *normal Christian life* cannot hold the weight of what God is about to do. Our wineskins must change. There is very little of what we now know as Church life that will remain untouched in the next ten years.

Reaching the Maximum

It has never entered the mind what God has prepared for us while on this earth. His intent is grand. Instead of limiting ourselves by our imagination and experience, let's press on to a renewed hunger for things yet to be seen. As we pursue the Extravagant One with reckless abandon, we will discover that our greatest problem is the resistance that comes from between our ears. But faith is superior. And it's time for us to make Him unconcerned about whether or not He'll find faith on the earth.

The Kingdom is in the now! Pray for it, seek it first, and receive it as a child. It is within reach.

ENDNOTES

1. *Quenching the Spirit*, 55, by William DeArteaga—Creation House.
2. Ibid., 19.
3. An individual who believes miracles stopped after the first-century Church was born.

CHAPTER 14

LIVING WATER, RUSHING RIVER

When it's raining, how should we respond? *We ask for more.* Not merely for our own sakes, but for the sake of a parched world.

The most important thing that we need to remember during this outpouring of the Holy Spirit is *where* the rain comes from and what it is meant to accomplish.

Our world is a dry and weary land, thirsting for water—water that you and I offer.

You are filled with the water of revival. In fact, there is a River of Living Water inside of you, just waiting to be released.

This is the supernatural collision that creation has been groaning for: The rivers of Living Water being released onto the dry and weary land.

Scripture reminds us of the "dry and weary" reality we face on a daily basis.

O God, you are my God; earnestly I seek you; my soul thirsts for you; my flesh faints for you, as in a dry and weary land where there is no water (Psalm 63:1).

In fact, when reading passages like Psalm 46, we can directly relate to the author's depiction of a shaking, troubled world:

God is our refuge and strength, a very present help in trouble. Therefore we will not fear though the earth gives way, though the mountains be moved into the heart of the sea, though its waters roar and foam, though the mountains tremble at its swelling (Psalm 46:1-3).

The good news? We are not left without hope. Right after the psalmist confronts us with the upheaval taking place on the planet—waters roaring and mountains trembling—he provides Heaven's timeless response to the chaos: *"There is a river whose streams make glad the city of God, the holy habitation of the Most High"* (Ps. 46:4).

Where does this River flow out of today? Most certainly it flowed *down* from the throne room of God on the Day of Pentecost.

If you have received Jesus Christ as your Lord and Savior, you have living water dwelling within you. Jesus made this clear during His discussion with the woman at the well. She was talking natural water, while Jesus was standing there, introducing her to a superior Wellspring of life.

Jesus said to her, "Everyone who drinks of this water will be thirsty again, but whoever drinks of the water that I will give him will never be thirsty again. The water that I will give him will become in him a spring of water welling up to eternal life" (John 4:13-14).

Every Christian is filled with living water. Now, it's time for that living water to become a rushing river!

Later on, in John 7, Jesus spoke of another expression of living water. This is where we presently are in God's unfolding timetable. Even though the water has been given—the Holy Spirit—it is time for us to ask for a fresh immersion in this life-giving torrent. It's one thing to have the Spirit living within you; it's another dimension to have Him resting upon you. For us to see an increase of revival and outpouring, we need to collaborate with the Spirit of God to see the One dwelling within us actually released through our hands, our words, our feet, our compassion, our prayers—*everything*.

> *On the last day of the feast, the great day, Jesus stood up and cried out, "If anyone thirsts, let him come to me and drink. Whoever believes in me, as the Scripture has said, 'Out of his heart will flow rivers of living water.'" Now this he said about the Spirit, whom those who believed in him were to receive, for as yet the Spirit had not been given, because Jesus was not yet glorified* (John 7:37-39).

Creation is waiting for the sons and daughters who carry the outpouring of Holy Spirit.

It's you. It's me.

It's our time.

It's the church's greatest hour to arise and shine in the midst of a dry, weary and shaking planet.

The rain of revival is falling.

The Holy Spirit Spirit is brooding, searching for vessels who willingly carry His Presence into their everyday lives.

It's time to ask for more.

It's time to see the living water within us become a rushing river outside of us, pouring Heaven into earth through Spirit-empowered sons and daughters of God.

READY FOR THE RAIN

I want the concluding words you read in this volume to be a Scriptural announcement of promise. Revival is not up in the air—it's very much at *hand*.

> "*The rain and snow come down from the heavens*
> *and stay on the ground to water the earth.*
> *They cause the grain to grow, producing seed*
> *for the farmer and bread for the hungry.*"
> —ISAIAH 55:10, NLT

This gives us a powerful picture of what attracts the unusual rain of outpouring and revival: *ready* ground. Yes, there is a strong element of God's sovereignty involved, where He alone decides the details of how these unusual visitations of His Presence manifest.

At the same time, there is something that mankind can do on earth that provides a setup for the great global outpouring of the Spirit that we are crying out for. We can be ready. We can do the works of revival—preach the Gospel, heal the sick, cast out demons, love the unlovely, give to the poor, carry the Kingdom into our spheres of influence, walk in the gifts and fruit of the Spirit. Basically, all "normal Christian life" kind of activity. We do what we *know* to do, stewarding the Holy Spirit, whose divine Presence lives within us.

While we steward His Presence, we also cry out and contend for the supernatural atmosphere that dwells within us to powerfully impact our communities and our nations. This is what's happened over the years. A man. A woman. A church. A community. Often a small group or a remnant. *Someone* who was being a faithful steward of the Holy Spirit's Presence in his or her life decided that was not enough. It was glorious, but not enough. It was sacred, precious and priceless—but not enough. Why?

These individuals were gripped by *what could be* on a greater level. They tasted realities of the Spirit that ruined them for anything less than outpouring of biblical proportions. What they experienced of God's manifest Presence compelled them to cry out for *more*—ask for the rain. Results?

The Protestant Reformation that opened eyes to the simple, but utterly profound truth of "saved by grace *through* faith."

The one-hundred-yearlong Moravian Prayer Movement that, in the spirit realm, birthed the very revivals and awakenings that were to come.

The Great Awakenings that swept across America's soil, confronting immorality in the world and complacency in the church. Through the thundering voices of John Wesley, Jonathan Edwards, George Whitefield, and Charles Finney, the Gospel spread across the land like wildfire.

The Welsh Revival of 1904 that saw a country radically impacted by a move of God which had both spiritual and socio-economic impact. A recorded 100,000 souls were ushered into the Kingdom, and their conversions dramatically impacted the culture of Wales.

The Azusa Street Revival of 1906, that birthed a movement of Spirit-empowered Christianity that has seen over 500,000,000 people across the earth taste of Heaven's fullness and release God's supernatural power on earth.

The Hebrides Revival in 1949, that brought an entire region under the manifest Presence of the Holy Spirit.

The great revival movements of the 1990's—Toronto, Brownsville, Smithton—that introduced a new generation to the "more" of God and birthed global missionary efforts that have seen millions come to Christ.

This is a mere sampling of unusual outpourings of the Spirit over the centuries. With each example, there were individuals who were stewarding the Spirit's movement in their lives, while also crying out for more.

Their stewardship prepared rain-ready ground for the Spirit to move in unusual, dramatic ways.

Now, a generation of rain-ready ground is being cultivated. This is not a statement of spiritual hype—it is absolutely factual. In the midst of global crisis and darkness, a great light is arising. There are stadiums being filled with Christ-followers, crying out for Holy Spirit revival in prayer. There are individuals who have taken Jesus's instructions quite literally and are healing the sick, prophesying and sharing the Gospel *wherever* they go. There are missionaries marching forth into the darkest regions of the planet, carrying the hope of the Gospel, while there are also missionaries being raised up to shape culture through Kingdom service.

As we faithfully steward what He has already given us—the Person of the Holy Spirit—let us likewise be faithful to pray for an unusual visitation of Heaven on earth.

May this great outpouring be a catalyst that disciples nations and prepares the way for Messiah Jesus to make His triumphant return.

It's raining. *So ask for the rain.*

God's already moving. *So let's ask for more and position every area of lives to experience this inheritance of revival and outpouring!*

ABOUT THE COMPILER

Larry Sparks is passionate about seeing Christ-followers—individually and corporately—experiencing the fullness of the Holy Spirit. To this end, he equips believers to cultivate revival lifestyles where God's supernatural Presence and power become the norm, not the exception.

Through training sessions, lectures, conferences and church services, Larry provides opportunity for people to experience the manifest Presence of God, while providing revelatory and biblically sound teaching on practical "how-to's" of igniting personal, corporate and regional revival.

Larry is a regular blogger for Charisma Magazine, author, co-founder of Renewing South Florida, and is the Publisher for Destiny Image publishing house. He has appeared on TBN, CBN, Cornerstone TV, *The Line of Fire,* and Sid Roth's *It's Supernatural* and holds a Master of Divinity in Church History from Regent University.

Contact: lawrencesparks.com

DESTINY IMAGE BOOKS BY LARRY SPARKS

Breakthrough Healing

Breakthrough Faith

The Fire That Never Sleeps
(with Michael Brown and John Kilpatrick)

ABOUT THE AUTHORS

ABOUT DR. MICHAEL L. BROWN

Michael L. Brown holds a PhD from New York University in Near Eastern languages and literatures and is recognized as one of the leading Messianic Jewish scholars in the world today. He is the founder and president of FIRE School of Ministry, host of the nationally syndicated daily talk radio show *The Line of Fire*, and the author of more than twenty books.

Contact: askdrbrown.org

DESTINY IMAGE BOOKS BY DR. MICHAEL L. BROWN

The End of the American Gospel Enterprise

Our Hands Are Stained with Blood

What Ever Happened to the Power of God?

It's Time to Rock the Boat

How Saved Are We?

The Fire That Never Sleeps

ABOUT BILL JOHNSON

Bill Johnson is a fifth-generation pastor with a rich heritage in the works of the Holy Spirit. Bill and his wife, Beni, who are senior pastors of Bethel Church in Redding, California, also serve a growing number of churches that cross denominational lines, exhibit power, and partner together for revival. The Johnsons have three children and nine grandchildren.

Contact: bjm.org

DESTINY IMAGE BOOKS BY BILL JOHNSON

Hosting the Presence

Releasing the Spirit of Prophecy

Dreaming with God

Strengthen Yourself in the Lord

The Supernatural Power of a Transformed Mind

When Heaven Invades Earth

ABOUT JOHN KILPATRICK

John Kilpatrick is the founder and senior pastor of Church of His Presence in Daphne, AL. He is an in-demand speaker, author, apostolic leader, and has had the privilege of pastoring two powerful revivals: The Brownsville Revival and Bay of the Holy Spirit Revival.

Contact: johnkilpatrick.org

DESTINY IMAGE BOOKS BY JOHN KILPATRICK

When the Heavens Are Brass

The Fire That Never Sleeps

ABOUT TOMMY TENNEY

Tommy Tenney is the author of the multimillion-selling *The God Chasers* series. He is the founder of GodChasers Network, a mission's ministry organized to assist pastors globally and distribute his teachings through various media. The Tenneys reside in Louisiana with their three daughters, son-in-law, four grandchildren, and two Yorkies.

Contact: godchasers.net

DESTINY IMAGE BOOKS BY TOMMY TENNEY

God Chasers

Open Heaven

ABOUT JAMES GOLL

Dr. James W. Goll is the founder of Encounters Network, Prayer Storm, and the God Encounters Training eSchool. James is an international best-selling author, a certified Life Language Trainer, and has taught in more than fifty nations. James was married to Michal Ann for thirty-two years before her graduation to Heaven in the fall of 2008. James has four adult children who are married and a growing number of grandchildren. James makes his home in Franklin, Tennessee.

Contact: encountersnetwork.com

Prayer Storm website: prayerstorm.com

DESTINY IMAGE BOOKS BY JAMES GOLL

The Seer

Dream Language

Prayer Storm

The Lost Art of Intercession

The Lost Art of Practicing His Presence

The Lost Art of Pure Worship

Elijah's Revolution (with Lou Engle)

ABOUT BANNING LIEBSCHER

Banning and his wife, SeaJay Liebscher are the Directors of Jesus Culture, a ministry mobilizing a generation of revivalists and reformers who will shape culture and transform nations. They are the Senior Leaders of Jesus Culture Church located in Sacramento, California. Their passion is to see nations awakened to the love and power of God and for a generation to fully give themselves for the cause of Christ in the earth.

Contact: jesusculture.com

DESTINY IMAGE BOOKS BY BANNING LIEBSCHER

Jesus Culture

Journey of a World-Changer

About Corey Russell

Corey Russell serves on the senior leadership team of the International House of Prayer of Kansas City and is an instructor at International House of Prayer University. His mission is to disciple and train young preachers and leaders. He travels nationally and internationally, preaching on the knowledge of God, intercession, and the urgency of the hour. He and his wife, Dana, have three daughters, Trinity, Mya, and Hadassah.

Contact: coreyrussell.org

DESTINY IMAGE BOOKS BY COREY RUSSELL

The Glory Within

Ancient Paths

ABOUT DON NORI SR.

Don Nori Sr is a driven man. The same passion that arrested him over forty years ago is still the primary, overshadowing power in His life. Along with Cathy, his wife of 40 years, they pursue life enthusiastically in the beautiful Cumberland Vally of central Pennsylvania. They spend much of their time blissfully spoiling their grandchildren and enjoying their sons and their wives. Don will probably write as long as God gives him breath.

Contact: donnorisr.com

DESTINY IMAGE BOOKS BY DON NORI SR.

The Forgotten Mountain

Manifest Presence

God: Out of Control, Out of the Box, Out of Time

Breaking Generational Curses

The Voice

The God Watchers

Secrets of the Most Holy Place

Breaking Demonic Strongholds

Romancing the Divine

Tales of Brokenness

How to Find God's Love

You Can Pray in Tongues

Supernatural Destiny

Yes! The Prayer God Loves to Answer

The Love Shack

A PASSIONATE, PROPHETIC SUMMONS
TO **PRAYER** AND **FASTING**

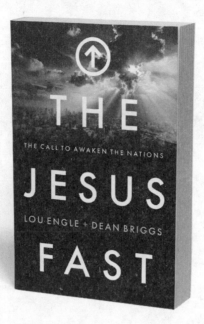

We are poised at a key moment in history. Amidst pain and chaos, we can turn the tide of evil in our lands. With excitement and profound insight, seasoned prophetic leader Lou Engle shows how: through bold faith and aggressive, passionate prayer and fasting.

Here he equips you with the dynamic, practical tools you need to answer the call of countercultural consecration. Using Jesus as the role model, he reveals that 40 days of prayer and fasting always precede breakthrough, revelations of God's glory, breakage of demonic hindrances, and more. As we join together in fasting and intercession, we'll see victory in the critical issues of our day—and we'll awaken the nations for Christ.

Global revival and transformation is imminent. Will you answer the call?

THE FORGOTTEN MOUNTAIN TRILOGY

The Forgotten Mountain

— BOOK ONE —

There is a reason believers struggle more than they should. There is a reason that there is so much pain, loss and heartache. It is not because we are destined to suffer because we are not. It is because we have forgotten the Mountain of the House of the Lord, the place of true inner governance under the rule of our King. He must increase and we must decrease. The Canaan life style is waiting as surely as it was waiting for ancient Israel to cross the river Jordan. We reign when we die...to ourselves.

After Pentecost

— BOOK TWO —

When ancient Israel fled the bondage of Egypt, they found solace in the wilderness. But it did not last long. They wandered in the waste places and wondered why it had to be so. But it didn't have to be so. They were called to pass through the wilderness as are called to pass through Pentecost into our Canaan in this life. Who will have the courage to leave the familiar, the secure, the visible evidence of His presence, opting for the authentic inner governance of the King; the establishing the permanent throne of His Kingdom within?

An Uncommon Revival

— BOOK THREE —

The lifestyle of the believer in Canaan is far different from the lifestyle of the wilderness that the ancient Israelites experienced. It is also far different from the life experienced in Pentecost. In this dimension of life, the King reigns, His presence tangible from within and the attributes of the King flow like water from the surrendered life. Here, destiny is fulfilled, the contribution of every man is appreciated and authentic Divine harmony begins to flourish among men.

EXPERIENCE REVIVAL
EVERY DAY!

Perhaps you've had an encounter with God that powerfully impacted your life. But then over time, the fire of that initial experience faded, leaving you wondering: *Is it possible to experience revival every single day of my life?*

The leaders of the Brownsville Revival and the Bay of the Holy Spirit Revival offer guidance to ignite and sustain your passion for Jesus.

Get ready to live passionately for Jesus, walk out God's divine purpose for your life, and enjoy His presence on a daily basis.

IT'S TIME TO REVIVE YOUR FIRE!

BUY NOW!

Available everywhere books are sold

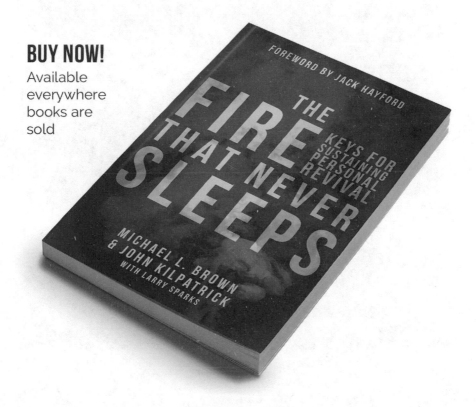

Get
FREE
E-BOOKS
every week!

LOVE □□
to READ club

JOIN *the* CLUB

As a member of the *Love to Read Club,*
receive exclusive offers for FREE, 99¢
and $1.99 e-books* every week. Plus, get
the **latest news** about upcoming releases
from **top authors** like these…

DESTINYIMAGE.COM/FREEBOOKS

**T.D.
JAKES**

**BILL
JOHNSON**

**CINDY
TRIMM**

**JIM
STOVALL**

**BENI
JOHNSON**

**MYLES
MUNROE**

□□ **LOVE** to **READ** club

 DESTINY IMAGE